Dear

White

Women

Dear White Women

LET'S GET *(un)*COMFORTABLE
TALKING ABOUT RACISM

SARA BLANCHARD & MISASHA SUZUKI GRAHAM

FOREWORD BY TERRI E. GIVENS

THE
collective.
BOOK STUDIO

Library of Congress Cataloging-in-Publication Data available.

ISBN: 978-1-951412-31-9
Ebook ISBN: 978-1-951412-43-2
LCCN: 2021902202

Manufactured in the United States of America.

Cover design by Andrea Kelly.
Interior design by Maureen Forys, Happenstance Type-O-Rama.

The Collective Book Studio
Oakland, California
www.thecollectivebook.studio

10 9 8 7 6 5 4 3 2 1

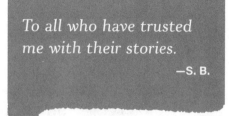

To all who have trusted
me with their stories.

—S. B.

To those who are, or
remind me of, my why.

—M. S. G.

Contents

Section III

ON BEING A NON-BLACK PERSON OF COLOR IN AMERICA

Foreword

The third decade of the 21st century has started with a mind-numbing series of violent events and trauma. The murder of George Floyd, a contentious election, and the January 6 attack on the U.S. Capitol, as legislators were certifying the presidential election, left many of us in shock. For the African American community, it was a reminder of hundreds of years of trauma that have led to a society that remains mired in structural racism, often marked by violence.

As we experience these events, it is important that we cultivate allies who understand the broader impact of our ongoing fight for equality. This book is an important step on the path to creating change, developing trust, and eventually, reconciliation. Reading this book by Misasha and Sara made me realize that I couldn't ask for better kindred spirits. Phrases like "looking inward," "respectful dialogue," and the understanding that "racism is largely baked into our society" are ideas that play an important role in my own anti-racism work. This book emphasizes the importance of allowing ourselves not only to get uncomfortable, but also to use our relationships to create change. It is through our personal connections that we can practice empathy and take action.

It is in my nature to be collaborative, and I love the fact that Misasha and Sara demonstrate the power of coming together as allies to address structural racism. Black men and women have carried the burden of fighting for civil rights and dealing with injustice for too long, and although there have always been allies, we need more. We need every person who cares about social justice to take up these issues, because we are once again at a critical juncture for the future of our children, this country, and the world.

Storytelling is central to anti-racism work. For African Americans, being able to tell our stories is important not only for understanding ourselves, but also for helping others to have empathy. However, stories and empathy are not enough. For hundreds of years, we have been fighting the scourge of structural racism. We must honor those who have sacrificed their safety and their lives to create change. We cannot be complacent about the challenges we are facing.

This book provides clear steps that White women (and men) can take to create change—not by being White saviors, but by using the privilege they have to empower others of all races and ethnicities. It starts by changing ourselves. The organizing principles of Listen, Learn, and Act that form the foundation of this book mesh very well with my six steps to radical empathy:

1. **Being willing to be vulnerable:** Allowing ourselves to be vulnerable means looking honestly at the ways that structural racism impacts each of us, and how that manifests itself in our daily actions.

2. **Becoming grounded in who you are:** By focusing on the truth of who you are, it is easier to become open to the ways that others are impacted by societal forces.

3. **Opening yourself to the experiences of others:** In order to have empathy, we have to be willing to consider that others have experiences that are different from our own, and that we must be intentional in trying to understand our differences. It means avoiding making assumptions about people, and being willing to listen and to learn.

4. **Practicing empathy:** We have to be intentional and work at trying to see things from someone else's perspective.

5. **Taking action:** What can you do to bridge divides? Start by looking at your own actions, whom you connect with, how you show kindness.

6. **Creating change and building trust:** It can start with small steps, but it is important to show that we are willing to get out of our comfort zone to create change.

White women are a critical component to change in this country. I have seen White women in my own neighborhood mobilize to support progressive organizations and political candidates. We have marched for Black lives right here in our own suburban neighborhood. Despite the pandemic, we have worked to forge new relationships and alliances. What I have found is that we energize each other. When I'm feeling depleted, I can turn to books like this to remind myself that I'm not in this alone. It is so important that we help each other carry the load, and I'm grateful for Misasha and Sara's work.

—TERRI E. GIVENS, author of *Radical Empathy:*
Finding a Path to Bridging Racial Divides

Introduction

*"Those who stand up for justice will
always be on the right side of history."*
—MARTIN LUTHER KING, JR.

There are certain moments in our history—both personal and textbook—that stand out as flashpoints, when something changes so quickly that it shakes our footing and threatens to change our lives forever.

The personal might be a sudden death in the family. An unexpected layoff. A business shuttered, unable to survive in changing times. Have you been there?

If so, you know that these flashpoints stop you in your tracks and force you to take stock of your life, reexamine your values, and decide how you will handle whatever it is you decide to do next, to make it through. You'll never be the same person you were before that moment.

Other flashpoints are those that we experience as a society, like 9/11, World Wars, and even the awful things that we have seen captured on cell-phone video and sent around the world.

The brutal murder of a Black man by a White Minneapolis police officer, who spent 9 minutes and 29 seconds kneeling on the neck of a fellow human being who was begging for his life and even cried out for his mother, brought the United States to its knees as it began yet another cycle of reckoning with race.

Although this wasn't the first murder of a Black man at the hands of a White man, nor will it be the last, the convergence of mass access to technology during a time when the world was shut down due to the coronavirus pandemic meant that George Floyd's murder took center stage in more minds than at other times in recent history. It was a collective flashpoint.

If you picked up this book, we're guessing that the developments of 2020 impacted you in some way and sent you searching for answers.

Maybe you're asking yourself how we as a country got here. Maybe you like the idea of being more anti-racist, to hold yourself and others accountable, but you're not sure where to start. Maybe this is the twenty-third book you've picked up this year, looking for the "best" way to understand other perspectives or a theory of racism that makes sense to you.

We know. We're there with you in the search for understanding.

We also know that this search can be overwhelming. You're suddenly attuned to every article that talks about racism and White supremacy and what White people can do better. You notice every time you see someone of color, wondering if you came across as friendly and accepting enough. You scroll through your social media feed and find yourself questioning the legitimacy, motivation, and truth of each post. You debate how to—or even if you want to—talk with your aging (or any) relatives about the inappropriate things that come out of their mouths.

You get tired.

Again, we understand. We get tired, too.

And you want to stop. It's very human to feel tired and want to stop, because racism is a huge, entrenched, complex issue to wrap your head around.

So here's why we're so happy you picked up this book: because it means that you're a good person, that you care about our world and the people in it, and that you want to do the best that you can. BUT, to be able to indulge that exhaustion and decide to walk away from the conversation? *That* is a privilege. It means that on a daily basis, race may not play a big part in your everyday life— that racism is something you don't *have* to think about. The truth is, Black people never get to step away from that conversation, because racism affects them every single day. And yet, let's be real, they're *more* exhausted by racism than White people. And we're here to say that this is exactly why you *should* read this book.

This book is here to make your search for change easier. In every chapter ahead, we give you practical steps towards becoming more anti-racist, so that rather than feeling reactive and rudderless due to the current state of the world, you can focus on implementing smaller, tangible action items in your daily life.

But along with that, we'll be emphasizing that this process is exactly that—a *process* that is an ongoing journey. That means we're not going to ask you to collect books on race that will gather dust on your bookshelf or tick boxes on an anti-racism checklist; nor will we ask you to throw up a black square on social media and call yourself "woke."

In other words, joining us on this journey toward being more anti-racist is an intentional life change. It's a change based not solely on those academic theories that you'll get from other books on this topic, but also, very importantly, on practical daily attitudes and actions.

This journey seeks a shift toward a goal, but one that cannot be clearly achieved. Setting a goal with regard to anti-racism is sort of like setting a goal to get healthier. Is there a magic weight or cholesterol number or amount of water you can consume that will make you "healthy"? Not really. It's a continuous process that we strive to embrace and stay in; we don't simply stop once we feel like we have achieved our goal.

Anti-racism is something we need to keep working on, whether it be in small conversations, like those we model for you in this book, or in commitments to finding ways to do our part to change the big structural problems.

Going back to those flashpoints for a second, we've had them throughout human history. Nazi Germany. Stalin's Russia. The Cultural Revolution in China. Slavery. The list is long. And so often we hear people discuss those periods with the firm belief that they would have been on the "right side" of history.

They say they would have stood up firmly for the marginalized, the oppressed, the people whose lives were being lost or destroyed and those who were being treated like animals—or worse. But history suggests that's not exactly the case. It's easy to see the wrongs in our rearview mirror and theorize that we would have been strong enough to stand for justice, for humanity, for all people, even when it would have been extremely dangerous to do so.

Today, we're facing another flashpoint moment. You have a choice to take a stand for humanity, to fight every day to be more anti-racist, to speak up for those of us who are marginalized, to make sure all rights are protected. Or, you can sit back, stay quiet (because it *is* safer that way), and hope that you won't be judged for your lack of action.

So our question for you is—what side of history will you be on? You've got the chance *right now* to pick humanity and take that stand, regardless of how challenging, tiring, or uncomfortable it may be. The history books are being written. Are you in?

Great. Now, who are we?

Misasha

Recently I was asked about my name and its connection to my identity. As you can imagine, when your parents give you a name they made up, you face a lifetime of answering questions about it (on a good day) or defending your right to be called what you would like to be called, rather than whatever name (or combination of syllables, or shortened version) makes the person asking feel more comfortable (on a bad day). As a result, I've thought a lot about my name, and what's in a name. So this time when I was asked, I didn't even hesitate before I said, "My name is a perfect representation of who I am." Here's why.

I was my parents' first child—the firstborn of a Japanese immigrant father and a White American mother. I am a child of lawyers and historians and teachers and storytellers. It was only fitting, therefore, being a biracial child, that my parents looked for a name that they thought would help me "fit in." They thought all Japanese would think the name they invented was Japanese, and all Americans would think it was American. You know what they say about best-laid plans, right? Yeah. As it turns out, pretty much all Japanese think it's an American name; and, because I don't look very Japanese, Americans tend to go down a deep Eastern European rabbit hole. I'm not from Russia, despite what my name might suggest. I have also been considered "exotic" or "nebulously ethnic." When you are always being positioned as "other," you start to think of yourself that way. So the need to figure out where I fit in and the desire to bridge cultures and communities have been central to my existence from my very earliest memories. If you've ever been to a rest stop somewhere in the United States and desperately looked for your name in those racks of little keychain nameplates, only to never find it, I think you might understand.

It is probably this sense of trying to fit in, or my acute consciousness of being biracial, that led me to spend as much time in Japan as possible, including working there after college graduation and again during law school summers. It is probably that same sense that led me to the practice of law and which propelled my specific desire to balance intellectual property litigation with pro bono aid for people who are struggling to be heard in our justice system. It is definitely my experience with fighting and struggling to fit in and be heard that led me to this point with Sara, first starting our podcast *Dear White Women* and now writing this book together. Because in so doing, I am literally fighting to save my children's lives.

For those of you who think I might be being dramatic, I understand. I may have thought so myself, many years ago, before I married my husband, who is Black, and had my two sons, who are multiracial but seen by the world as Black. There have been many points in my life where I have benefited from White privilege (see Chapter 1, "Excuse Me, I Don't Have White Privilege," page 17) even though only my mother is White. There have been exactly zero times when my husband has benefited from those privileges. He, and my sons, live under a constant reminder that, as Black men in America, they are considered "less than."

I was pregnant with my first son when Trayvon Martin was shot and killed in the street by an armed so-called vigilante. He was seventeen years old. I was holding my second son in my arms, a tiny infant, when Tamir Rice was gunned down at the age of twelve for holding a cap gun. When you have Black children, every story that you hear of a Black person being killed is one that you add to your mental catalog of "this is how my child might be killed." When George Floyd was being murdered in the street and called out for his mama, I heard my kids calling my name. This thought breaks my heart in ways that I cannot physically write or describe. But in that same instant that my heart is breaking, it also gives me the strength to fight, because as a mother, you WILL fight to save your children. You will do *anything*. This book is part of my *anything*.

(Another thought that breaks my heart is imagining being a Black mother who has to carry a mental death catalog like this while also trying to figure out how to navigate her way through a world that is stacked against her own survival.)

Having conversations with Sara and with other close friends and family has reinforced for me that a mother's fears for her children and her family are the closest to her head and heart. However, I found that once one starts thinking more broadly, about the fears and hopes of those who may have different narratives and different experiences in the very same place where you live, or work, or love—it's hard to stop. But I get it . . . I understand why that kind of perspective is often in short supply, why the dialogue stalls. Those conversations are hard to start. Especially if in your circle of friends, or in your family, everyone is the same race—when would you even have the opportunity to engage in discussions about the hopes and fears bound up in issues of race?

That's why I'm here to tell you this, which may provide you a little bit of food for thought: This past summer, I took my sons to a peaceful Black Lives Matter rally. We made posters before the event. My elementary school–aged son, after writing "Black Lives Matter" on his poster, then wrote, in smaller letters underneath, "My Life Matters." So to return to this central question: why do I do this work? Because I want us to get to a place where no kid feels the need to justify his life to a group of people who may want to take that away from him simply because of the color of his skin.

I know we are capable of doing hard things. I'm asking for your help to save my children's lives, and the lives of all others who look like them. We can do this together.

Sara

To some degree, I feel like a fraud being here. I'm not Black, nor am I related to anyone Black. I'm Japanese and White and am married to a White Canadian man with White-presenting children living in a predominantly White state.

Who am I to be teaching you about race, racism, and how to be more anti-racist?

Maybe that's a thought that keeps a lot of people silent. Can you relate? But since childhood, I have always prided myself on standing up for what I believe is right, both for myself and for society at large. I got my otherwise peace-loving self into a shoving match in elementary school standing up to a girl who was being a jerk to a classmate; I wrote my college entrance essay on why we each need to do our part against drunk driving. I like to think of myself as a kind, considerate, thoughtful person who stands up against injustice and speaks up for what I believe is just. So as a person with friends and loved ones who are constantly faced with racism, who am I NOT to be learning, talking about, and doing something about a system and mindset that pervades our society and hurts our fellow citizens every day? Racism will not go away if we as non-Black people don't decide to participate in making change.

And I think the hardest, most important step is taking a look inward.

I would have loved to think that because I'm biracial, I can't be racist. I'm the product of a Japanese immigrant mother and a White father. I was born and raised in the suburbs of New York in a home that bridged cultures, with after-school activities that included tennis, tap dancing, Japanese tea ceremony, piano, and calligraphy lessons. I never got to do Girl Scouts or soccer or sleepovers on Friday nights like the other kids, because my Saturdays were taken up by Japanese weekend school. (Now that I'm bilingual, I owe my mother an apology for the countless tantrums I threw on the kitchen floor.) My blond-haired, blue-eyed father would look me straight in the face when I sassed my mother about the rules she imposed on me that seemed more restrictive than those my American peers had in their homes, telling me in no uncertain terms that I was expected to respect her and the culture she was raised in. I certainly grew up knowing that there is more than one perspective in life.

During college, I sang in a gospel choir that celebrated Black culture. But during my time there, tensions flared between people who had different feelings about the purpose of the group—celebrating Black students at Harvard—conflicting with the reality of an increasingly non-Black membership. That tension forced uncomfortable conversations and decisions about who could stay and who should leave, and was my first experience with having really jarring conversations about belonging.

I resided for years in Japan and Hong Kong and New York, places with long histories that are open to many different ways to live. I've sponsored music groups that address racial and gender identity on tours through school districts, organized conversations with mixed-race company in my home, created panel discussions for predominantly White communities to listen to the experiences of their Black members, worked on video projects showcasing voices of Black people in America, cofounded and cohost the racial and social justice podcast *Dear White Women* with Misasha, and have many Black friends.

But the reality is, none of those things make me "woke." **None of them make me not racist.** (I especially protest the line of reasoning that if you are a non-Black person who has Black friends, it means you are not a racist.)

Why? Because I think racism is largely baked into our society. If we are really honest, we have to admit that we still often have knee-jerk reactions when we see people who look different than us. It's human; we are attracted to similarity, we feel that people who are similar to us are actually better than those who are different. (To see support for this, read about the elementary school red shirt/blue shirt experiment on page 25.) That's on the personal level; that's not even talking about the structural biases that are perpetuated in many public and private institutions in our country.

And *this* is why I'm qualified to be here in conversation with you: because I largely identify as White. After spending the first half of my life in metropolitan, cosmopolitan areas, including living abroad, I've now spent nearly fifteen years living in predominantly White areas with my White husband and White-presenting children. My Asian identity is still a core part of my values, but my Japanese flag-waving has largely faded. Misasha has even caught me referring to "us" when I talk about White people.

Any of us can hold up highlight-reel stories about how amazingly open-minded we are, but there's always more to do. More to think about. Room to grow. Ways to make our personal world more diverse, inclusive, and beautiful.

The biggest thing I want to say is that I'm here *with* you, not here to judge you.

I don't believe there is such a thing as arriving at "woke." Work in this realm is a continuum, a spectrum, a progression, a direction we are moving in towards being more anti-racist. I have been working on myself and my community now for years.

Why has this taken on more urgency as I've gotten older?

It's astonishingly simple: because I'm largely spurred on by the stories you just read from Misasha, my best friend—mainly about how *her* fears about her kids being killed based solely on the color of their skin were so drastically different than my fears for my lighter-skinned kids. Honestly, I've always cared about anti-racism, but not enough to *do* something about it until it became personal.

I hope we can help you find a personal connection to it, too.

You Bought This Book. Now What?

Back to the two of us. The way we work together is to be both really practical and really personal.

There are a lot of other incredible books and articles out there that we'll refer to during the course of this book if you want to dig more deeply into the history or the theories of race, racism, and anti-racism. To be sure, there are powerful actions we can take to help dismantle the systemic racism that's embedded in our schools, prisons, banks, and more.

But we think that the only way to make change last is by coming at it from two directions—top down and bottom up. For the purposes of this book, we focused on the bottom up: the personal actions you take every day and how you can work to identify, address, and change them intentionally.

Because at the end of the day, dismantling systemic racism is NOT an easy task that'll go smoothly. It is messy and uncomfortable for everyone involved. As a result, everybody working on this complicated process needs to start with a good hard look at themselves and the choices they make on a daily basis, and to identify the powerful *why* behind their involvement in the work. Because otherwise, at the first bump in the road, it all becomes seemingly too difficult and we're more likely to give up.

To be clear, a *why* is NOT a *should*. It's not motivated by guilt. It's what you care about, of your own free will.

And the reason that we need to talk about this with other non-Black people, and in particular women, is because the why behind change is often deeply personal. It's grounded not only in fact, but in relationships—and we, as women, know that we value those relationships in ways that are both immeasurable and powerful.

We also know that these conversations about race don't frequently happen in nondiverse circles, and yet sometimes we reside almost entirely in those very circles. So part of our collective why behind this book, and driving the work that we are doing, is to make change by getting uncomfortable together in our small spheres of influence. Those can be book clubs, parent email groups, exercise classes, coffee dates, and so many other spaces. And now that we have outlined all of this, we have a question for you.

What's *your* WHY?

What made you pick up this book? Who do you know who's affected? Why do you give a hoot about anti-racist work?

Write it down. You can do it in pencil if you want; you can do it right here:

_____

_____

_____

_____

Or you can write it on a sticky note and put it somewhere else, or go to your journal. But write it down so you can see it, and take a look. Is that truly your why? Is there something, someone, who will be even more deeply motivating for you? Give it a moment. Breathe it in.

We want you to hold that thought in your heart throughout the course of reading this book and throughout all the days and years to come. That's your why, and that's what's going to power you through when reading about another injustice done to a Black person nearly breaks your will to keep going.

Okay. Now about this book.

The book is organized by what we call "pain points," scenarios you might run into or conversations you might stumble across where your gut instinct fires in every which direction, signaling that something isn't right here—but you don't know what to do or say.

We know you're busy AND that you want to start changing the world around you, so the segments are laid out in fairly short chapters. We want you to be able to pick the book up and put it down and pick it back up again without feeling like you need to reread everything until that point.

Within the realm of social change, we think there are three important verbs to keep in mind.

listen

It's a learned skill to listen to people's stories. People are the experts in their own lives, and we need to believe them when they tell us what's going on for them. So we endeavored to bring you a true story to illustrate the point we were trying to get at within each pain point.

learn

There is a whole sordid history in our country that isn't taught equally throughout the states. Depending on where you grew up, for example, slavery might have been mentioned three times in your history textbook, or over one hundred times. We make sure all the basics are covered in each pain point, so you understand the facts and history around each topic. No #fakenews here.

act

It's well enough to say we're nice people, that we listened, that we learned, maybe we even shared a story on social media about racism—but what changes if we don't do anything with that information? Nothing. We recommend at least one or two things you can do or say differently in each scenario. These might be words to stop using (not to be obvious, but never, ever, ever use the N-word—more on that in Chapter 9, page 101) or things to start doing. There are places throughout the book where we suggest something you may want to write down; we created a downloadable PDF journal that includes some prompts, which you can find on our website, dearwhitewomen.com, and print yourself a copy.

All of these subsections are included in every chapter to guide us in giving you a well-rounded picture of the topic within. These three concepts are by no means a complete capture of all the problem (and growth) areas you'll face in your journey towards anti-racism, but they are the most common and useful forces we have found in our years of conversation and from the research we put into this book.

Along with the organizing principles of Listen, Learn, and Act, we also interspersed boxes in pertinent places describing what we identify as "microaggressions"—small acts or remarks with often unintentional hurtful effects. These are designed to give you that moment to pause, reflect, and understand for yourself why the impact of a few words or a simple act upon the listener or receiver may be so much more painful than the responsible party intends—after all, it's the impact that we are concerned about.

We really hope that you'll take what we say to heart, and that you'll feel like you have found here, perhaps after a long search, a practical set of things you can do differently in your daily life to make you feel like you're on the path toward being more compassionate, understanding, and educated about people who might not look like you but are human beings just like you.

We are all worthy of respect, and we are so glad you're here with us. Let's get started.

On Being White in America

SECTION I

CHAPTER 1

Excuse Me, I Don't Have White Privilege

John is a White man, an airline pilot, and on his off days, he goes running in the neighborhood for exercise. In the summer, he goes in the morning or evening when the temperatures are cooler; in the spring or fall, he might go in the afternoon when the sun feels just right. He doesn't really think about *when* he is going, other than when it is convenient for him and feels good. When the time comes, he throws on whatever exercise clothes are clean—his preference is usually some combo of readily available dark blue, grey, or black clothing—laces up his shoes, tucks a key into his inner pocket, and is off. It's great to see him when he gets back from working up a good sweat; Sara can sense the exhilaration he feels after his freedom to just take off and get away from the kids for a bit, to do what he wants for an hour. It's so healthy.

As women, we get jealous of our male counterparts' freedom. What we wouldn't give to feel like we could go out in the twilight of dawn or at dusk or any time we want, and not worry that somebody is going to get creepy or attack us! The Central Park jogger story and others like it lurk in the back of our minds. So we settle for going on walks with our friends, or heading out over a lunch break when many other people are out, walking their dogs or walking to meetings. And of course, we always take our phones with us. If we were to sense danger, we can handle it by making an immediate call to the police.

This is why hearing Antonio's story was eye-opening for us.

listen ————————————————————————— 👂

Antonio Wint is a Black man, a father, and the successful owner of an IT company. He told us about what it takes for him to get out the door to go for a run.

Remember John's sense of freedom and ease? Not so much for Antonio. The mental hoops Antonio has to jump through seem countless compared to anything John or we have had to consider.

First, he picks a time. Early morning and late evening are out, because with the dim lighting, Black skin is considered more of a threat. He has to work during the day, and ideally he can get out for a jog during his lunch break. That doesn't always happen, though, so more often than not, it's an early evening run right after work before it gets too dark.

Second, he has to choose his clothes. Even if it's cold, hoodies are never an option. He purposely picks bright-colored clothing—clothes that make it clear that he's okay being seen and remembered. Clothes that indicate that he is exercising and not running away from a crime scene.

Third, he lays out his route. He has already turned on phone tracking so that he can be tracked by his family on his run. He tells his wife and child that he's going to be gone for thirty minutes, along a route that they already know. He will let them know if he changes his route along the way, making a right turn here or a left turn there. On his way out, he tells them that if he's not home in forty or fifty minutes, to begin looking for him and check the tracking on his phone.

Fourth, if he cannot be tracked down, he reminds them, they should consider calling the police.

Lastly, only after he has taken all of the steps above, he finally takes a deep breath and heads out the door JUST TO GET SOME EXERCISE.

Now, you may be thinking we can dismiss this as just one man's experience, but know that we've heard many more stories like it—a Black woman who wears neon outfits so passersby in her Southern

White neighborhood can't deny seeing her, a Black man who makes sure he wears a helmet each time he rides his bike so nobody accuses him of stealing it. This need to think and plan for other's perceptions of you is not unique to Antonio; it's something many, many Black people go through every day just to get out their doors.

We've heard well-intentioned White people say that Black people are overreacting by feeling such fear, and to that we say: People are experts in their own stories and fears. Telling a person they shouldn't be afraid or that they're overthinking something is dismissing and dehumanizing their very real concerns.

We're able to empathize with this. If you are a woman and you've ever been afraid to do something—wear a short skirt, drink a little too much, walk home alone late at night—you know what it means to be barred from opportunities based solely on your appearance. You lose the opportunity to experience freedom of expression, freedom of consumption, freedom of simply existing in a public sphere at a certain hour without feeling like you might be blamed for an action taken against you. And it's incredibly frustrating when a man tells you you're overthinking it, that nothing is going to happen, that you're being silly by worrying about these things. Just like it's incredibly frustrating for Black people when White people tell them that nothing will ever happen and to get over it.

Remember that Ahmaud Arbery did everything that Antonio has been doing for years—wearing bright exercise clothing, running in the middle of the day, on the streets not too close to any personal homes in a "nice" neighborhood—and he was *still* killed, hunted down like an animal by three vigilante White men. Stories like Ahmaud's—and so many others like his—strike fear in a Black person's heart, because they realize that they're doing everything in their power to be seen as a human being who is simply existing in the public sphere, and yet, they can still become a target. (You can hear more of Antonio's story in his own words by going to voicesfromnextdoor.com.)

To check our intuition, we asked John—the White male jogger—if he's ever felt like he was a target based on the color of his skin. Without skipping a beat, he said no, that he's never felt a threat or even like he's missed out on anything based on his appearance.

This is what we are talking about when we talk about White privilege. White privilege is referring to NOT being barred from an opportunity based solely on the color of your skin.

White privilege is being able to go jogging in a nice neighborhood without a second thought.

White privilege is being able to ride your bike without your helmet, and not feeling like someone will call the police on you for stealing it.

White privilege is not having your résumé tossed out because your name is too unique . . . is not being the only person who looks like you in a room or store or meeting . . . is not having to search far and wide to buy books for your kids with illustrations of characters that look like them. It *is* having your White children get the benefit of the doubt more than kids whose skin is darker; it *is* your White kids being able to learn about their race in school all year long instead of being relegated to one special theme month; it *is* feeling protected by the police rather than having to speak with your kids about how to show deference and caution around them.

MICROAGGRESSION: Claiming "I don't see color"

White privilege is also being able to say you're color-blind. To people of color who experience bias nearly every day, from micro to small to large aggressions against them, the world is not color-blind. Even if you *yourself* claim and honestly believe that you don't discriminate, society doesn't often take the time to get to know Black people as individuals; as a whole, society so often sees them as part of a stereotype. Only people who have the privilege of not experiencing racism or don't know people who experience racism are able to talk about being color-blind with a straight face.

Additionally, every time someone says they are color-blind, they are taking away a part of a non-White person's identity. For example, Misasha's kids are proud to be Black, Japanese, and White. They've been taught to be proud of their skin color as a reflection of who they are. If you say you don't see color, you're taking away that pride. That part of their identity. And we think that's quite the opposite of what people intend when they say "color-blind."

White privilege is both a legacy and a cause of racism. To understand and change anything in the realm of anti-racism, we need to start there.

learn

Where does White privilege stem from?

Well first of all, please take a seat. Breathe for a minute, because we just unloaded a lot of information. If you're a parent, it's possible you feel a little heavier thinking that you and your kids might live a little differently than those human beings we heard about, Antonio and his wife and child.

You are not at fault for this.

But if you identify as White, you do benefit from the privilege that has been assigned to people of lighter skin tones since the foundation of our country. We need to understand and accept this before we move on, because this is the foundation of all anti-racism work.

When we talk about White privilege with White people, the instant reaction is usually some sort of recoil. Denial. Anger.

"No, I don't have White privilege," the story often goes. "I grew up poor and we had to work super hard to get everything we have."

We hear that. We know that. We see that many people work extremely hard to get where they are, and that effort is something to be proud of!

In the context of this conversation about race, though, it's critical that we not make the mistake of assuming that privilege means *financial* privilege.

White privilege is referring to not being knocked down several pegs based solely on the color of your skin. It's the privilege we have in this country to *not* be discriminated against simply because we are White, compared to the many forms of unfair treatment experienced by people with Black (or Brown) skin.

While it may seem obvious on the typed page, the call to acknowledge White privilege is often met with resistance. To address that resistance, let's first get clear about hierarchies. Since racism is the belief that certain races of people are by birth and nature superior to others, and we are addressing how Black people in our country face racism, then, by definition, some grouping of people is "more highly valued" than Black people. We have to accept that that group is White people.

It's painful to think that we might possibly be complicit in a system like this—one where Black people are worth less than White people. *We weren't part of the system of slavery,* we want to shout. *We didn't create this hierarchy!*

We all want to feel like we are good people—and according to the research, feeling like a good person has a lot to do with how we are seen by others. But while research suggests that our first instincts lead us to behave with cooperation rather than selfishness, we also know that when people are anonymous or unlikely to be caught, when they're distanced from real people, they're less likely to do good. How many times have you been driving and seen someone flip someone off, or not let someone merge? Bad behavior behind the wheel is easy because we're isolated and fairly anonymous in our cars. In the realm of cyberspace, we've all seen nasty Facebook comments or hate speech or cyberbullying. It's societal pressure from real people that keeps us on our best behavior, or at least behaving as though we are "good."

The truth is, as humans, we prefer to be in community with others. Do you remember how it felt during the COVID-related shutdowns, when many people were cut off from their usual human interactions? Loneliness—the distressing feeling that accompanies the perception that one's social needs are not being met by the quantity, or especially the quality, of one's social relationships—has proven to be negative for people's health, both physically and mentally.

We think about the conversation we had with Marcus Bullock, founder and CEO of Flikshop, about the eight years he spent in a federal prison from the time he was fifteen years old—a child who made a really bad decision and who had to pay the price for it as an adult. One of the primary motivators for his business, a software company that builds tools to help families send postcards to their incarcerated loved ones, is to help keep individuals in prison cells connected with their families and friends, so they can maintain their humanity and hope. The unfortunate reality is that people who get entangled in the criminal justice system are seen as having violated moral norms, and therefore they're often not only legally barred from rejoining certain groups—as voters, employees, students—but are also often socially ostracized from all the groups they were part of prior to incarceration: family, friends, church, HOAs, schools. To avoid loneliness, it's not uncommon for formerly incarcerated individuals to gravitate towards each other, forming a group with people who have also experienced time in the system.

What that shows us is that humans are motivated to maintain membership in groups, and to feel like we can make meaningful contributions to those groups that are important to us—contributions that are aligned with the values of those groups. If we identify strongly with our church community, we prioritize attending church on Sunday. If we belong to a hiking group, we honor nature and its conservation. If we identify as staunchly Republican or staunchly Democrat, oftentimes instead of voting by issue or by candidate, we vote down party lines.

How does this propensity to want membership in groups apply to this conversation about race and racism?

White people are a group. But we're trapped in a dichotomy of wanting to believe we are good people and wanting to maintain our relative privilege, so we hide acknowledgement of our White privilege. We'd rather deny that White privilege exists—because if enough individual White people deny it, then it truly does become invisible on a societal level, and that invisibility protects both the privilege and the sense of innocence members of that group enjoy.

How do we hide White privilege? Consider how often we identify ourselves as White. When we are talking about identity of any sort, are we naming Whiteness outright—in the same way we'd identify someone as Black, or Asian? If not, White people have the privilege of being assumed to be a "default" race, the standard against which all other races are measured. Now let's consider how many people of color we have in our "favorites" list of contacts on our phones. Do we actively have Black friends? How often do Black children come over to our homes for playdates? When we are not involved in circles that include people from different ethnic backgrounds, we can remain blind to the advantages we have, because we simply don't see—or hear about—those racial inequalities firsthand.

But let's try not to feel defensive. It is possible that you are a White person who has many, many friends of color. And contrary to well-trodden progressive beliefs, not having that many Black friends—living in segregation—does not mean we are "bad people" or have any ill will towards people who look different than we do.

Taking a look at the country as a whole, data aligns with the insular nature of the contents of many of our phone contact lists in terms of race. While studies show that segregation peaked in the 1960s and 1970s, approximately 13 percent of today's United States population are Black people—so how many of that 13 percent live in our city, our town, our block?

According to a report following the 2010 Census, "the average White person in metropolitan American lives in a neighborhood that is 75 percent White. Despite a substantial shift of minorities from cities to suburbs, these groups have often not gained access to largely White neighborhoods. For example, a typical African American [person] lives in a neighborhood that is only 35 percent White (not much different from 1940) and as much as 45 percent Black. Diversity is experienced very differently in the daily lives of Whites, Blacks, Hispanics, and Asians."

Additionally, despite the 1954 landmark Supreme Court ruling in *Brown v. Board of Education*, which declared that racial segregation in schools is unconstitutional, in 2020, more than half of American schoolchildren were in racially concentrated districts where over 75 percent of students were either White or non-White. And our public schools continue their slide toward re-segregation: They are less integrated now than in 1970, when court-mandated school desegregation busing began. (For more on this, see Chapter 15, page 154.)

If we live in an area where there is not a large concentration of Black people, the easy and most common default is to be friends with those who are around us who look like us. A study drawing on contact theory found that schools that have moderate levels of heterogeneity—moderate mixing of the races—had high levels of friendship segregation, but that once schools were really, really mixed, interracial friendships became more of the norm. We can probably extend that study to real life, and say that unless there is a fairly evenly mixed racial population in our circles, we are more likely to be friends with people who are of our same race.

Even further to the point, in another study, the team at Barna asked 1,000 people whether their current friends are "mostly similar to themselves" or "mostly different from themselves" in a number of areas. The majority chose mostly similar for:

- income (56 percent vs. 44 percent)
- political views (62 percent vs. 38 percent)
- religious beliefs (62 percent similar vs. 38 percent different)
- education level (63 percent vs. 37 percent)
- life stage (69 percent vs. 31 percent)
- social status (70 percent vs. 30 percent)
- race or ethnicity (74 percent vs. 26 percent)

So while our friends are likely to think and live similarly to ourselves, in this study, race proved to be the most common factor in finding social membership.

If our inner circles are largely comprised of people of the same race, with similar social status, income, and religious beliefs as us, what happens?

Honestly, we don't often question it. In fact, we might even think it's great—we feel like our group is better than others. Yuck, but yep. We as humans have what is referred to as an "in-group bias."

To test this theory, psychologist Rebecca Bigler conducted the red shirt/blue shirt experiment in the early 1990s. She asked elementary school teachers to talk about children's shirt colors the way they would typically speak about gender ("Good morning reds and blues, let's sit red-blue, red-blue. What a good blue group member"). The teachers remained unbiased, fair, and never linked the groups to traits—and yet after three weeks, the blue shirt children thought the blues were better; the red shirt children thought more highly of reds.

If we have any sense of identity around the people in our lives that make up a kind of membership defined by regular social interaction—that is, if we have a strong social circle that is largely homogenous—our tendency is to think more highly of our own group. That's how humans work.

So if a large group of us look and act and seem similar enough, we tend to be very proud of our group identity. To justify that pride, we often emphasize the effort we put into our own lives to work hard and make a good life for ourselves, perhaps a better one compared to our childhood, and we want to be credited with that effort. We want to be proud of our individual work. Unfortunately, the easy extension of that thinking—because we tend to be in segregated areas largely surrounded by our likenesses—leads us to this: We believe that if *we* were able to be successful, *everybody* should be able to "pull up their own bootstraps" and get the same result. That's the myth of the American Dream, where we think we all have the freedom to pursue prosperity and success for ourselves and our children, if only we work hard. White people certainly don't want to think that we are at any advantage, because we worked *hard* and have felt uncomfortable and faced adversity in our lives. It must mean that others—in particular Black people in other communities—simply aren't working as hard, because they don't live where or how we are living. What's wrong with that?

Everything. Because there is an historic reason for segregation and disparity in the United States. Black Americans have not experienced the same freedom to pursue their prosperity and success that White people have.

act ————————————————— 📢

So how do we address the widespread denial of White privilege? We begin by owning our identity.

While it's easy not to think about racism if we don't grow up or live around a lot of people of color and people from different backgrounds, at the very least, we can't escape mention about people of color outside our spheres—in the news, for example, or in movies and TV. If you identify as White, do your part in acknowledging Whiteness as just as significant of a race as Blackness. How do you start? When you begin talking about your perspective, have a mental mantra that acknowledges your own identity—something like, "as a White middle-class heterosexual woman" or "as a White cis-gendered essential worker"—so you acknowledge the impact that your race, gender identity, sexuality, and class may have on your perspective.

Another thing you can do is identify your pronouns under your name in your email signature (and maybe even an explanation as to why you're doing this). While it's not directly linked to race, being proactive with your identity labels reinforces that others are free to assert theirs, and that you are open to the reality of multiple identity narratives—one of which, of course, is race.

Then, listen to people.

Listen to people like Antonio. People like so many other Black Americans living in their skin who are hoping we'll listen to their struggles, their fears, their pain. Empathy is the experience of understanding and sharing the feelings of another, and that empathy helps build a more sustainable foundation to this work. It lets us connect with another human being's experience and understand that we as people are not all treated the same. Look for tips on page 43 about what it takes to practice active listening—listening with empathy without letting our defensiveness get triggered (what is commonly referred to as "White fragility") and what to do in those moments when defensiveness (often involuntarily or to our own surprise but almost inevitably when facing certain challenging concepts and discussions) rears its ugly head.

But if we're honest, we know this listening part is also where we can run into a problem.

Do you know how to access stories from people who don't look like you? Do you have a Black person in your life you can speak with about race? There are a lot of people who don't. You might find yourself in this situation.

As we mentioned earlier, there are a lot of areas in this country that are still segregated. Or maybe there was only one Black person in your grade, or one Black family in your community, and because they were the one outlier, it seemed like they were not treated differently, that everybody got along, leading you to grow up thinking racism isn't really a problem in our society.

Luckily, nowadays, we have technology on our side. We are able to access the multitude of voices on social media platforms: We can watch *Voices from Next Door*, listen to or watch *Uncomfortable Conversations with a Black Man*, or read the *Black Moms Blog*. Follow intentional community organizations like The Black Man Can, which humanize Black people. Listen to their stories.

We encourage you to begin connecting with these stories, because this is where you might encounter a moment that will trigger your *why*. We spoke in the introduction about the importance of identifying why you are interested in being part of the anti-racism movement, because it's a long, tough road. If you love someone who is Black, it's not a road you can just step off of—Misasha can't, and by extension, Sara can't. But we don't want you to feel like it's too hard, so you do step off—we want you to have a real connection with somebody who you are motivated to make changes for. Perhaps once you have that connection, you'll be able to challenge the implicit bias, that gut reaction you have to a Black person you haven't met yet. For now, we want you to feel the humanity of a person who doesn't look like you and understand their dilemmas and their pain.

CHAPTER 2

White Privilege— A Deeper Dive

Even without personal connections to a Black person's experiences, it's possible to have eye-opening moments about privilege. We have to seize those moments with some internal reflection and be willing to learn more.

listen

Our friend Brad shared his story as an example.

Brad grew up White in the northwestern United States. His father was full of confidence in the American Dream, thanks to opportunities that opened to him from wealthy, powerful mentors who saw him as someone they could trust. Brad grew up absorbing his dad's worldview, thinking that anybody can achieve success if they put in the effort.

A few years ago, the doors to Brad's perspective were blown off when he watched an animated video on Facebook that showed the difference between a White versus Black reality. In the video, he saw a White child graduate from high school, get accepted to a prestigious college (in part because his father graduated from that same college), and get an internship at his father's friend's firm. In contrast, the Black high school graduate's parents didn't graduate from college, so he wasn't given any college connections or career opportunities.

MICROAGGRESSION: Asking a Black high school student to clarify whether he got into Stanford or Stamford

"I recognized my own life in that video, the power of those connections," Brad shares. "Even though I didn't have connections in my chosen industry [video production], the clients I got first came through family and friends." Those connections set him up to have a portfolio of work that he could then show to an ever-growing number of clients. In more recent dealings in his adult life, he realized that while he doesn't feel ashamed of having opportunities, he does recognize that not everybody has them—that sometimes, Black people have to work at least twice as hard as he does just to make a living.

Not everybody wants to hear, or accept, Brad's realization about inequalities tied to race. However, digging into the history of our country can help us understand where he's coming from. Let's take a look at how we got here.

learn————————————————

There are plenty of books that we can reach for to dive into the history of this country, but the super short primer—some of which we'll get more into later in the book—is the following:

The founding fathers of our country were rich White men who owned land (and probably some slaves along the way). We talk about voting in this country as if it's some sort of privilege that everybody has access to, fundamental to our citizenry. But the truth is, some of the framers of the Constitution didn't trust "regular people"—i.e., people who were NOT rich, White, male landowners—with the power to decide the electorate, so the right to vote wasn't even in our original Constitution. It's only through *constitutional amendments* that we are given the "equal" right to vote. Classism was built into the foundation of our country.

We cannot forget the reality that slavery existed, either. In 1619, the privateer White Lion brought twenty African slaves to the British colony of Jamestown, Virginia. By 1787, with nearly 40 percent of the Southern population consisting of enslaved people, the Constitution was forced to recognize the institution of slavery, counting each enslaved individual as three-fifths of a person for the purposes of both taxation and the electoral college. Over 246 years, millions of Black people were enslaved until they were theoretically freed by the Emancipation Proclamation in 1862, followed by a more certain end to slavery with the 13th Amendment after the Civil War in 1865.

To put this in perspective, realize that as of the year 2020, Black people have been "free" for 155 years—compared to the 246 years they were enslaved. An entire population of millions of people were set free from their masters and plantations after a lifetime of no education and no connections, and were told to go make something of themselves. They were even told to get a job or else risk being ensnared in the system of Black Codes—which is where, immediately after the Civil War ended in 1865, many states required Black people to sign yearly labor contracts, and if they refused or were not able to find a job, they risked being arrested, fined, and forced into unpaid labor.

Imagine being born into your family, possibly torn away from your parents and siblings, being made to work from the time you're a child and told that it's illegal for you to learn how to read or write. And then, one day in your teens or early twenties, you are next told to go figure out your life—and if you don't, you will be "unofficially" put back into a system of restraint and subjugation. Where would you begin?

Wherever you started, it definitely wasn't as a wealthy and educated person. So imagine, just a little over one hundred and fifty years ago, newly emancipated Black adults in this country were nevertheless poor and uneducated, through no fault of their own, and starting from scratch. And state laws to restrict the former slaves' freedom called Black Codes immediately sprang up to keep them from rising above. These were soon replaced by Jim Crow laws, spurred by the interpretation of the 14th Amendment as "separate but equal" treatment of the races—which meant unequal access to everything from homes to hospitals to courts to shops, and implemented legalized racial segregation.

By the late 1800s and early 1900s, Jim Crow laws strictly limited opportunities for Black people in the United States. Black people were prohibited from entering public parks; segregation was enforced for things including public drinking fountains, waiting rooms, hospitals, building entrances, schools, and neighborhoods. You certainly couldn't marry someone of a different race.

Then, in 1934, the Federal Housing Administration (FHA) was created by President Franklin D. Roosevelt. The FHA institutionalized the system of discriminatory lending in government-backed mortgages. Developed by the Home Owner's Loan Coalition (HOLC) in the 1930s, government surveyors graded neighborhoods, putting them into color-coded maps indicating the level of security for real estate investments in 239 American cities. The maps were based on assumptions about the community, *not* on the ability of various households to satisfy lending criteria. Here's how those maps were color-coded:

- **A (green)** were new, homogenous areas ("American Business and Professional Men"), in demand as a residential location in good times and bad.

- **B (blue)** were "still desirable" areas that had "reached their peak" but were expected to remain stable for many years.

- **C (yellow)** were neighborhoods that were "definitely declining." Generally, sparsely populated fringe areas that were typically bordering on all-Black neighborhoods.

- **D (red)** (hence the term "redlining") were areas in which "things taking place in C had already happened." Black and low-income neighborhoods were considered to be the worst for lending. Loans in these neighborhoods were unavailable or very expensive, making it more difficult for low-income minorities to buy homes.

The institutionalization of these practices is the most shocking part. Filling in racial status wasn't at the discretion of the individuals who were filling out the forms on behalf of the bank; it was something they were *required* to indicate, right alongside average lot size. For example, part of the form asked for "Percentage of Negro infiltration," including a number from 0 to 100. Or, for occupation, bankers might write "professional executives" for the

A neighborhoods and, with one exception, "Negro" for the Black inputs. As if being Black was an occupation!

Despite *Shelley v. Kraemer*, a 1948 case in which the Supreme Court ruled that racial covenants were unconstitutional, the discriminatory practices captured by the HOLC maps continued until 1968, when the Fair Housing Act banned racial discrimination in housing.

Again, let us insert a reality check: Looking back from the year 2020, the banning of racial discrimination in housing was enacted only fifty-two years ago. The parents of our middle-aged friends had to deal with redlining in their own lives. Think for a moment about the conversations our generation's White parents were having around the dinner table when they were children; think now about the conversations our Black peers' parents had to have around the dinner table at that time. They were probably very, very different because the laws governing their lives were very, very different.

The longer-term impact of redlining lasts to this day. A study by the National Community Reinvestment Coalition shows that the vast majority of neighborhoods marked "hazardous" in red ink on those maps in the 1930s are much more likely than other areas to comprise lower-income, underrepresented residents today. On the flip side, 91 percent of areas classified as "best" in the 1930s remain middle-to-upper-income areas today, and 85 percent of them are still predominantly White. Change is slow—very, very slow when coupled with systemic racism and generations of discrimination.

With housing creating one of the biggest opportunities for building wealth in the United States—an opportunity that has not trickled down equally by any means to the Black individuals in our country today—this goes a long way in explaining the huge disparity in wealth between White and Black families. In 2016, according to Brookings, the median net worth of a White family was nearly 10 times greater than that of a Black family.

Now we know why the disparity and segregation we see today in our states, cities, and communities is the way it is. It's not because Black people are any less intelligent, ambitious, trustworthy, or hard-working than White people are, but because they started off on much worse footing and had to live with many more restrictions than our White ancestors did—systemically. It's not easy to make huge leaps in one generation alone. For that reason, we have to see the "exceptional" Black individuals in our society—President Barack Obama; Oprah Winfrey; Antonio Wint, CEO of his own company; Caylin Moore, a Rhodes Scholar who grew up in Compton—as just that. The exceptions.

MICROAGGRESSION: Telling a Black person that they're articulate or that they "speak so well"

It is slow progress, two steps forward and one step back, to make meaningful, significant change, and that is why we say that the anti-racism journey we are embarking on has to be positioned as long-term and sustainable.

If you identify as White and are entering this anti-racism conversation, here is something to keep in mind: The segregated communities we live in allow us to remain blind to our own advantages, because we don't see the racial inequities that exist as we go about our daily lives.

Unfortunately, even if you did grow up poor, even if you are still struggling to put food on the table, if you present as White in America, you experience White privilege in relation to Black people in this country who live in a system that was designed for and continues to put them at a disadvantage.

Yikes. So what can we do about White privilege?

act

Most powerfully (but rhetorically, because he's part of the anti-racist movement now), Brad asked the question, "How do we give people those opportunities they might not otherwise have?" It's a great question, and one that is mindful about addressing racial disparity with the right intention. This isn't about "saving" Black people. White saviorism assumes, insidiously, that other races don't know how to help themselves, so White people are here to do it for them. (You might sometimes see this referred to as the "White savior industrial complex." This describes organizations created by White people that attempt to solve what the organizers perceive to be the needs of communities that they are not a part of.) What we want to be is supporters, allies, activists—so if you're not sure what someone might need, or what the solution is, ask people before making assumptions. We all know our own stories the best.

But we *can* use the power of our privilege to amplify the stories and the work of marginalized people. In Brad's case, using his natural skills and career as a filmmaker, he and Sara co-launched *Voices from Next Door*, a local video project based in Denver for which they interview their Black neighbors, recording their "real life stories about the way race plays a part in everyday life in America."

What are YOUR superpowers? Your spheres of influence, your skills that you can use to advance anti-racist work? Are you a boss who leads conversations by naming the key descriptors of your identity and encourages others to do the same? Can you begin buying products and services from businesses owned by Black people—from the candles you use to scent your home to the catering trucks you hire for corporate events? Are you in a position to do away with referral bonuses, because we tend to recommend people just like ourselves (i.e., White)? Do you have capacity to be a mentor to someone who doesn't look like you? Could you speak up (repeatedly, if necessary) at your local PTA or board meeting to demand conversations addressing racism and anti-racism and encourage diverse membership?

Even if your superpowers do spring to mind right away, know that doing the small things matters too. Sometimes they matter even more, when done often. For example, we should speak up when people make racist jokes; we can interrupt when people ask us to "stop being so political" (we'll talk about that more in Chapter 3, page 37).

Bottom line? Owning our White privilege begins with understanding and accepting that White skin has an advantage in this country—or, at the very least, that it's not a disadvantage. Before we consider supporting policies that can make racial equity possible—policies that are pitched as controversial, like reparations, #defundthepolice, and even affirmative action that so many women benefited from and yet vote against—we need to first acknowledge our position of advantage.

It may feel difficult, but if you identify as White, consider writing in your own hand on the line below: "I have benefited from White privilege." It may seem pointless in the privacy of your home and these pages to pen this statement, but science shows that writing things down helps encode thoughts in our long-term memories, and helps us internalize feelings and focus on the truly important things. Acknowledging White privilege is a fundamental part of White people's participation in anti-racism work, so if you're game, please take this very important step with us.

_____

_____

_____

CHAPTER 3

Oh, Stop Being So Political

One of the most common pushbacks we hear when people bring up the topic of racism is that it's not an appropriate topic for the space. Say it's in an exercise group, or a parenting group, or LinkedIn, or at the dinner table; you'll almost always hear somebody say "stop being so political, this space is for us to all feel good together."

That kind of thinking leaves us scratching our heads. One group of people thinks we are talking about making the space good for all people *including* people of color; the other thinks race is political and should therefore be barred from civil discourse. Who's right?

listen

Kendra, a White woman, had a side gig as an independent wine seller. In the shockwaves after George Floyd's murder, when there was a surge in White people paying attention to racism against Black people, the CEO of the wine company she worked for sent out an announcement to the company about the sizable donations she was making to the NAACP and BLM.

It backfired.

Kendra told us that several consultants quit, arguing that BLM is a hate group and that they couldn't work for a company that would make such a controversial donation. Other executives analogized that donation with one that might have theoretically been made to the Trump campaign; they said a business cannot take a political stance, especially when that business consists of independent consultants, because it's not permitted to speak for all of those people. With all of the pressure from within her company, in the end, the CEO rescinded the BLM donation and donated $50,000 to the NAACP.

Hold up.

Why is Black Lives Matter seen as a political organization? According to their website, the #blacklivesmatter global network "builds power to bring justice, healing, and freedom to Black people across the globe." It's about restoring humanity, dignity, and civil rights to Black people. But in some circles, BLM is championing changes that many take to be political. (For more on Black Lives Matter, see Chapter 10, page 109.)

How do we address the blurred line between humanitarian concerns and political issues, so we can actually talk about the things that matter?

learn

Politics vs. Humanity

Strictly speaking, "politics" refers to anything relating to the government or the public affairs of a country. It is something relating to the ideas or strategies of a particular party, or group, in politics. The term "political issues" can refer to controversies debated within the political system—everything from divisive social issues such as abortion to taxation and government spending to foreign policy and free trade.

Concrete examples of political issues might be things like, should we levy another school tax this year? Do we need a light rail for our city? Should we increase (or decrease) taxes?

Political issues also include more controversial questions like, should gay couples have the same adoption rights as heterosexual couples? Should the government increase (or decrease) environmental regulations to prevent climate change? Should women have the right to choose to have an abortion?

Phew. Yeah, those are all political conversations.

On the other hand, "humanity" refers to the core values behind the principles guiding attitudes, perspectives, individuals, organizations, institutions, constitutions, and law-making concerned with a humanitarian quality of life for all and encouraging all to treat others in a humane way: being compassionate, sympathetic, and showing generous behavior or dispositions.

The United Nations laid out their understanding of and expectations for human rights for all countries—regardless of the political status of said country or territory—in their milestone document, the Universal Declaration of Human Rights of 1948.

The United Nations is an organization with 193 members from 195 countries in the world as of this writing—meaning, *it represents the majority of the world.* And according to the Universal Declaration, human rights include the right to life and liberty, freedom from slavery and torture, freedom of opinion and expression, the right to work and education, and many more. Some of the key articles about human rights that are relevant to anti-racism include:

> Article 4: No one shall be held in slavery or servitude; slavery and the slave trade shall be prohibited in all their forms.

> Article 5: No one shall be subjected to torture or to cruel, inhuman, or degrading treatment or punishment.

> Article 7: All are equal before the law and are entitled without any discrimination to equal protection of the law. All are entitled to equal protection against any discrimination in violation of this Declaration and against any incitement to such discrimination.

> Article 9: No one shall be subjected to arbitrary arrest, detention, or exile.

> Article 23: (1) Everyone has the right to work, to free choice of employment, to just and favourable conditions of work, and to protection against unemployment. (2) Everyone, without any discrimination, has the right to equal pay for equal work.

> Article 25: (1) Everyone has the right to a standard of living adequate for the health and well-being of himself and of his family, including food, clothing, housing and medical care, and necessary social services, and the right to security in the event

of unemployment, sickness, disability, widowhood, old age, or other lack of livelihood in circumstances beyond his control. (2) Motherhood and childhood are entitled to special care and assistance. All children, whether born in or out of wedlock, shall enjoy the same social protection.

Do those bring up any thoughts or feelings for you? For us, they certainly did.

Article 4: This says that slavery is not allowed, but our country was founded with slaves, and White people owned Black people for the next 246 years. We've never made amends in the form of reparations or otherwise for that, nor are we teaching this history adequately throughout the country so we don't repeat the same mistakes—or make blanket judgments about Black people out of historical context.

Article 5: If you've watched the 9-minute, 29-second video of George Floyd's death, you will have witnessed cruel, inhuman treatment. That's just one example of police brutality in the United States.

Article 7: Equal protection of the law seems more of a theory than an actual practice when we look at the imbalanced power that prosecutors have in courtrooms, or when it comes to composition of juries that don't equally represent Black defendants.

Article 9: The War on Drugs has created opportunities for arbitrary traffic stops that lead to unequal targeting of Black people (see Chapter 11, page 117) or, in border states like Arizona, empowers officers to make traffic stops that target people they thought were "likely" to be undocumented immigrants.

Article 23: Women are still paid less than men for equal work; Black, Hispanic, and Indigenous women are paid less than White and some Asian women.

Article 25: (1) The ever-widening wealth disparities in the United States mean more and more people have inadequate standards of living. The porous American healthcare system does not offer a safety net of security for everybody, only for those who are employed by companies that offer health insurance, and the governmental system designed to be that safety net implemented by President Obama is under attack. (2) America offers way, way, way less protection for maternal health and maternity leave compared to most developed nations in the world, and there's a tremendous disparity in protections for children in poor communities. Just think about the seven-year-olds home alone all day during the coronavirus pandemic, left to feed themselves and attend virtual school with poor Internet access while their parents go to work out of necessity.

When we look at how the United States historically and currently performs against a list of fundamental and widely accepted human rights, it's clear there is work to be done.

This is where distinguishing politics versus humanity gets tricky.

Paying women the same wage as men for the same job is not a political issue, it is imperative for honoring women's humanity; having some form of fundamental healthcare is not a political issue, it's a humanitarian right; and asserting that Black lives matter is NOT a political statement: It is a human statement.

However, when we discuss *how* we want to address these disparities, it becomes political. After all, as per the definition of politics, we generally need to rely on our government to make the necessary changes to address these problems.

Since when did talking about politics become taboo?

For a long time, according to our parents' generation, engaging in political debate was an earnest and lively intellectual process. Political conversations were largely filled with facts, logic, and thoughts informed by our values. Sharing conversations like this has been glorified in evocations like TV's *Mad Men* and many other stories and images in that spirit; it was a hallmark of civilized dinner table conversation.

However, over the last decade or so, it seems that it has become taboo to talk about politics. Around the time when the "middle" became less robust, and more extreme views on both the left and the right—exacerbated by polarized, drama-seeking 24-hour cable TV news—became more commonplace, it seemed any *discussion* about politics became more of an *argument*. It's human nature for people to want to avoid the discomfort of sitting in arguments, and so we started avoiding certain topics altogether.

Why did politics become so argumentative? One reason we can trace is shifts in the moral, intellectual, and cultural climate wherein politics went from something brain-centered, delving into how policies might affect our greater nation and society at large—out there, big picture, long-term—to something more heart-centered, personal, immediate, and emotional. People started identifying themselves by their politics.

At this juncture, it's interesting and helpful to look at the interplay between identity politics and religion in the U.S. and whether the former is in any way related to a significant decline in the importance of religion to this country's population. Ronald Inglehart and Pippa Norris have studied religious trends for decades, and note that "From 1981 to 2007, the United States ranked as one of the world's more religious countries, with religiosity levels changing very little. Since 2007, though, the United States has shown one of the largest moves away from religion of any country for which we have data."

It's significant that within our lifetimes, the United States has shown a marked decline in religion. Sure, as societies develop, people feel a lot more secure in their survival—they're not as likely to starve, violence and murder rates go down, and life expectancy increases—and as that sense of security rises, people tend to rely less and less on religion. That's what those who study these trends tell us, anyway.

But the United States has been developed for quite a while, so it's important to note the more straightforward political correlation that likely played another part in the decline of religion in this country. "Since the 1990s, the Republican Party has sought to win support by adopting conservative Christian positions on same-sex marriage, abortion, and other cultural issues. But this political appeal to religious voters has had the corollary effect of pushing other voters, especially those who are young and culturally liberal, away from religion." It once was generally assumed that religious beliefs shaped political views, not the other way around. But recent evidence indicates that causality can run the other way: Panel studies have found that many people change their political views first and then become less religious.

If Christian people, for example, accept the idea that women should have the choice to control their bodies or that homosexual people should be recognized in their unions just as heterosexual people are, then they are faced with having to resolve conflicting religious and political views. According to the studies, these conflicts will lead them to having to make a choice about distancing themselves from either religion or politics.

As we discussed in Chapter 1 (page 17), people want to belong to groups. In the situations above, people are being forced to choose between groups. We'd venture that once people make a choice, especially if they've left a religious group in favor of a different set of political values, they're likely to default even more strongly to our human tendency toward groupism—to think that their new chosen group is better than the former one. Thus political ideology becomes internalized; it becomes a personal representation of who we are, and by the natural workings of human psychology, we are typically compelled to think we are better than people in other groups.

Obviously there are many, many different types of people with different values and beliefs in the United States. Unfortunately, it's easy to forget that the functions of a government—politics— affect not just us individually but all the people in our country. Perhaps as we personalize something that by definition isn't and shouldn't be personal, we become too focused on assuming the side we come down on is right and the other side is wrong. We become too focused on *being* the right thing, at the expense of *doing* the right thing.

act

Let's start being MORE political, if it means we listen to other people's perspectives.

One of our kiddo's elementary school classes was told NOT to talk about who they would vote for during the 2020 election cycle so that they wouldn't hurt the feelings of other children in the classroom whose perspectives might be different. In contrast, our middle-schooler's class was encouraged to talk about who they would support and why—and to listen considerately to anybody else who thought differently. That was incredibly refreshing, a little bit unexpected, and something we encourage more people to get behind.

Having open conversations about politics and our beliefs might feel uncomfortable at first, but we have the choice to be respectful of other people's perspectives—even if we have leadership that doesn't—keeping in mind that being respectful does not mean avoiding asking questions or ignoring different points of view of the people around us.

Respectful dialogue does mean learning—and making sure we teach our kids—how to not only ask questions that will help us understand another person, but also deeply listen to their responses. What is deep listening? It's not preparing our responses while the other person is talking, for starters. But more than that, it is listening with the goal of developing empathy, trying to connect with and respect the other person and what they are saying; and many studies show that being open to listening to other people makes it more likely that they will reciprocate by listening to us as well. Simple as it seems, it's an incredibly powerful and hopeful way forward.

Extensive research in one of the studies mentioned above helped its authors identify four strategies for having more productive conversations about things we might disagree about.

1. **Acknowledge the other person's point of view.** We can do this by reflecting back on what they're saying with "I believe what you're saying is . . ." or "I understand that . . ." but even more importantly, the study's author emphasized the importance of saying "Thank you, because . . ." and explaining *why* it was important for you to have that conversation.

2. **Be a little less forceful in stating your claims.** Instead of using language that makes it sound like it's "my way or the highway," it's actually more helpful to phrase things in a way that makes it seem like you're open and receptive to another opinion, and may even be influenced by it. Insert words like "might" or "may" or "perhaps" instead of "absolutely," "certainly," or "always."

3. **Use positive language instead of focusing on the negatives.** We often default to telling people why their idea isn't going to work, but it's more productive if, again, we keep possibilities open by saying something like, "Let's consider the benefits of green," instead of "There's no way red will work."

4. **Highlight areas of agreement, no matter how small.**
   There are usually things—beliefs, values, or experiences—
   we can find that bring people together even in a difficult conversation so we feel closer and are reminded we
   share the same challenges and hopes. Despite the broad
   spectrum of reactions to masking up during COVID, for
   example, everyone could probably agree that we want the
   pandemic to end, and that the whole thing has been really
   hard to get through.

It comes back to remembering our common humanity and prioritizing that instead of getting caught up in the groupthink and
pride of the groups we might belong to.

Unfortunately, healthy dynamics and thoughtful strategies
like these are currently under siege in the United States. Research
from the Brookings Institution states that polarization "exacer-
bates intolerance and discrimination, diminishes societal trust, and
increases violence throughout the society. Moreover, it reinforces
and entrenches itself, dragging countries into a downward spiral of
anger and division for which there are no easy remedies." Though
the terrible rifts in society in the United States weren't created by
Donald Trump's divisive presidency, they were certainly exacerbated
by it and are likely to last long after his departure from power.

Countries that become increasingly polarized do not survive.
"Over the past four decades, the chilly chasm of negative sentiment
between Democrats and Republicans in the U.S. has nearly dou-
bled, and it has grown faster and larger compared to the partisan
climates of eight other established democracies analyzed in the
study."

We need to work—RIGHT NOW—to reestablish the robust
middle ground we've lost so that our kids can have a fighting
chance at a more united country. It is ideal to start them young,
by modeling these conversations in our own lives and encouraging
them to talk about their own views, too. Otherwise they'll grow up
and still find themselves in a country like the one we are in today—
or worse—where things like political talk in the workplace creates
15 percent more cynicism, 13 percent less productivity, and worse
work quality; where we have viciously divided elections; where we
judge people based on what sort of truck they drive or their gun

ownership status or religion or educational background. Let's do better for these kids of ours.

What do we say when people tell us to stop being so political?

The key thing? Remember that working towards anti-racism is about human beings, like Misasha's husband and sons—not about some politician. We are currently seeing more racism in response to politics—but racism has been happening for a very long time. Even though we're more aware of it right now, violence and discrimination and the disparate treatment of Black people has been happening for centuries. It's not about what political party is in power at any given moment, it's about humanity and doing what's right.

Does "Defund the police" seem controversial?

Sure, if you just focus on headlines. It leads people to believe proponents want to take money away from the police force entirely. But what the movement really wants is to reallocate the resources the police department currently receives to more mental health services, more appropriate non-lethal response teams, and better resources spread around for housing. This actually takes huge burdens off armed officers so they can address problems that are specific to their training and expertise.

Does looting suck?

Sure. And does the idea of violence and protests and destruction of property feel threatening? Absolutely. But we must recognize that there are people from all over the political spectrum showing up at these charged events, which then sometimes spin out of control and damage and looting ensue—in those moments it is far from a partisan thing that automatically means one side is right and the other side is wrong. Change is hard, and uncomfortable. The small changes in history are small changes; big change takes a lot of upheaval. Which is where we may be right now.

Because you know what truly sucks? That Black people are made to feel less than human. Not just because of the history of slavery in the United States, but because there are systems in place that continue to disadvantage them, along with widespread aggressions and microaggressions that continue to hurt them on a regular, individual basis. Being dehumanized sucks. THAT is the focus of #blacklivesmatter—undoing the dehumanization we have imposed on Black people. Each policy change they suggest can be discussed separately, but Black Lives Matter is NOT a political statement. It is a statement about humanity. It's about rehumanizing all of us so we can stop arguing across an artificial political divide and connect again—as people first, by having civilized conversations about our country and its communities that will benefit us all.

Continue pushing back, and encourage people to move beyond sound bites to sound analysis. Communication and understanding goes both ways, and we have to do our part to make it work.

CHAPTER 4

But I'm Not Racist

I f you were a human being in America during 2020, you probably asked yourself this question at least once:

Am I a racist?

And the answer was probably, "nah."

listen

This sentiment echoes the experience of our friend who told her mom that she believes everybody who grows up in the United States has some racism inside of them, and we have to figure out how to spot it and work against it. Her mom exploded in anger, shouting, "I'm sick of being called a racist! You don't know anything about me and what I've done in my life." Can you relate to her mom at all?

None of us want to align ourselves with the horrific images that come to mind when we picture someone who is racist. We imagine pitchforks, mobs, a lynching—Black men hanging from trees. Or we picture hate-filled White men spitting the N-word at someone who dares to come into their store to buy something. In other words, images of slavery, segregation, and people brutally opposing the Civil Rights fight.

Many of us have come to internalize that a racist is a BAD PERSON, because they dehumanize and attack fellow human beings.

But the truth is much subtler than that.

learn

The definition of a racist is "a person who is prejudiced against or antagonistic toward people on the basis of their membership in a particular racial or ethnic group, typically one that is a minority or marginalized."

An article from Learning for Justice, an organization with the mission of catalyzing racial justice in the South and nationwide, states: "As human beings, we are not naturally racist. But because of the way our brains are wired, we are naturally 'groupist.' The brain has a strong need for relatedness." (We'll explore this concept in more detail later.)

We are wired to group ourselves by similarities.

We want to find ways in which we are connected to people. We meet up with people whose kids go to our kids' schools; we find people who attend our churches, synagogues, mosques, or meditation centers. We connect with our neighbors, peers in our interest groups, college buddies, and office mates.

As discussed in an article published in Bloomberg CityLab, researchers found that "amid the total universe of all the people we know, we generally each have a very small inner circle. If you were to rank-order the people we talk to the most, the majority of our attention would be devoted to just a handful of friends or family." This study said that instead of a social circle, we have more of a social onion—a core group at the center, and many layers around it that build outwardly as we go farther from the core. For Americans, that core has, on average, 3.4 people—and for people from races across the board, nearly 2 of those 3.4 people consist of family members. Pausing for a moment, who is in your core group? What racial groups do they belong to?

If your core group is very homogenous, you're not alone. "Fully three-quarters (75 percent) of white Americans report that the network of people with whom they discuss important matters is entirely white, with no minority presence, while 15 percent report having a more racially mixed social network." Overall, it appears that White people are much more likely to have friends that are White—even more so than Black people have only Black circles (65 percent solely Black; 23 percent have a mix) or Hispanic individuals have solely Hispanic circles (46 percent solely Hispanic, 35 percent have a mix).

> **MICROAGGRESSION: Professing, "I'm not racist, I have a Black friend"**

The study broke this tendency for homogeneity down further to see if political orientation affected a social group's racial composition, and found that it did not make a significant difference whether a person in the core identified as Republican or Democrat. It also didn't make a difference if they identified as a White male or a White female—the ratios were about the same.

Does this high percentage of White people forming all-White social circles imply that most White individuals are biased—or is it because Americans live in such segregated communities?

The patterns of regional concentration by race and ethnicity have been shaped by history, based on historical patterns of migration. According to CityCommentary, "Blacks were brought to the Southern United States as slaves, landed primarily at places like Charleston, Tidewater Virginia and the Gulf Coast, and to this day, are disproportionately concentrated in the South. Most Latinos have migrated from Latin America, and are heavily concentrated in the Southwest. Asians have a disproportionate concentration on the U.S. West Coast. The patterns that were in place 100 years ago are still reflected today in the regional concentrations by race and ethnicity."

What effect does segregated living have on us as individuals?

Having lived in New York, then in Boston, Tokyo, and Hong Kong for the early part of her life, Sara grew up surrounded by diversity and socialized regularly with people of all different shades of skin. But for the past fifteen years, she has lived in predominantly White areas of the United States, so her real-life interactions have been mainly with White people. And the painful-to-admit truth of it is, whereas she never used to blink when she saw a Black or Asian person, Sara takes more notice now of those who are not White. It's human nature to default to noticing differences when we become used to a certain level of similarity in our surroundings. And because her kids' school friends and neighbors are predominantly White, it's easy for her to befriend those people and not seek out more diversity.

What does this suggest about Sara's relationship with racism? How can she possibly maintain empathy for someone who walks through society with different color skin if she doesn't have close interactions with them on a regular basis? If she weren't actively creating conversations about anti-racism, how easy would it be for her to get caught up in the White narrative about privilege not existing (that others should just work as hard as "we" do, or that they're playing the "race card" again)? In the absence of real-life interactions, is having digital relationships (via phone or Internet or social media) with multiracial friends from her past helping her stay informed enough about the range of experiences of others in the world?

The Internet actually makes our groupist tendencies worse.

Sara's parents had a long-distance relationship while one was living in Hong Kong and the other was living in Japan, and they often told their kids how lucky they were to be growing up in the era of email and the Internet, because *they* used to have to pay several dollars per minute (in the 1970s!) to make phone calls to keep in touch.

Surprisingly, though, as email and Internet technology has developed, the social media platforms that dominate it have led to an increasingly disconnected, segregated society.

The film *The Social Dilemma* features interviews with a number of the leading developers of the most common social media platforms that exist today: Facebook, Twitter, Instagram, YouTube, Google. Their vision in creating these platforms was to connect people across geographic distance and help them gain a more global understanding; they even created the "Like" button to "spread love and positivity in the world." But all of the developers interviewed in the film left their positions at these companies due to ethical concerns about the industry that they helped create.

It's the same old story: Social media businesses are built on making money through advertisements. For that reason, their computer algorithms are designed to maximize each user's eyeball time. More people being online means more money, so instead of being designed to support their original vision of human well-being, these platforms work to get users (us!) addicted to the platforms so that they stay there. (And these high social media profits come at an even higher cost to users: Instead of making us more connected, we may actually feel more alone. Studies have linked usage of the smartphone and social media to increased rates of depression and the skyrocketing suicide rates in the United States.)

How do they get us so addicted? They play on our psychology. They collect data on each "Like" that we click, what sort of posts we comment on, and how long we spend watching what type of videos—and then feed us more and more of the same. We might not even be aware of just how much we are spoon-fed content that already aligns with our own worldviews.

As we continue to be fed views that play into our groupings, similarities, and affinities online, our digital lives become parallel to our more homogenous social circles. Counter to social media's original vision of giving users a more global view of things, we fall into a self-perpetuating echo chamber where we begin to think most people must feel the same way we do. More and more, we are insulated from exposure to opposing viewpoints or from hearing about experiences different from our own. Instead, the feeds we are exposed to all seem to support what we think.

We are already wired as humans towards confirmation bias— meaning that we tend to hear information that confirms what we already believe, and we disregard information that goes against what we believe. We might not realize that this is what's happening . . . until we see that our Facebook feed is full of the same people's posts, even though we have several hundred other "Friends" on the site. Or, we open up our news app next to someone else, and see the differ- ence between the headlines that show up on our phones, all thanks to the clicks that we've made in the past.

We as a society are becoming increasingly divided, segregated into groups, as a result of both our geography and our technology.

Unless we consciously seek out perspectives different than ours, putting in the effort to balance our intake of information, we are being stuffed increasingly down a rabbit hole of our own making.

The media bias is affecting our perception of Black people.

As we've discussed, White people are already less likely to have a close social circle that includes other races, and their social media feeds are relatively self-affirming. In this context, then, it's important to note the role that traditional media plays in shaping our perceptions of Black people.

As it turns out, according to a study by Dr. Travis Dixon, news and opinion media are "almost 1.5 times more likely to represent a White family as an illustration of social stability than a Black family," doing things like overrepresenting Black family poverty while underrepresenting White family poverty, depicting Black fathers as absent in their children's lives, and overrepresenting the association between Black families and criminality while underrepresenting the association between White families and criminality.

These patterns of media representation promote antagonism toward Black males, present exaggerated or erroneous views of their tendency towards violence and criminality, and spur on public support for more punishment against them.

All of these things that we can consciously control—social circles, social media feeds, media representation—nevertheless lead to something even more disturbing: our unconscious bias against Black men. A study cited in the Opportunity Agenda's documentations of bias show that "the amygdala, a region of the brain that is associated with experiencing fear, tends to be more active when whites view an unfamiliar black male face than an unfamiliar white male face, regardless of their conscious reports about racial attitudes." Studies also found that images of Black men (even "seeing" unknown Black faces flashed at subliminal speeds too rapidly to consciously perceive) tend to bring up feelings of hostility in White people.

Yikes. It's pretty important to be aware that our unconscious bias can make us feel more hostile. Basically, as Zaretta Hammond notes, "a system of inequity is maintained by negative social messages that dehumanize people of color, women and LGBT people as 'the other.' For folks in the in-group, the brain takes in these messages and downloads them like software into the brain's fear system. This leads to implicit bias: the unconscious attitudes and beliefs that shape our behavior toward someone perceived as inferior or as a threatening outsider."

We all have implicit bias (or prejudice, as we "pre-judge"): This instinct helps us make faster judgments about our surroundings. Implicit bias is a survival trait, an unconscious way of keeping us safe. When we have a sabre tooth tiger coming at us, for example, we immediately recognize it as a threatening outsider, so we run away without a moment's hesitation.

> **MICROAGGRESSION: Crossing the street when a Black person is approaching you on the sidewalk**

Jennifer Eberhardt, a psychology professor at Stanford University who studies implicit bias, says, "You don't have to have a moral failing to act on an implicit bias." But there are times when making snap judgments can lead to bad decisions. The challenge is for us to become aware of our own implicit biases—shaped not just by inherent human survival, but by our past experiences, media, social media, and society—before we end up *saying or doing* something racist.

My social circle is largely White, and I have implicit bias. Does that make me racist?

Misasha had the opportunity to introduce Dr. Beverly Tatum on a webinar about anti-racism and children. Dr. Tatum used the following metaphor of a moving walkway during that event and it stuck with Misasha.

Imagine a moving walkway—those horizontal escalators you see transporting people through an airport. The walkway is moving in the direction of racism in the United States. It's *always* moving in that direction, as it's the way policies were set when this country was founded. An active racist is someone who is walking down that walkway, speeding along now because that person is not just riding toward racism but actively taking steps towards it. On the flip side, an anti-racist is someone who has turned around and is actively taking steps *away* from racism. You can imagine how slowly the anti-racist appears to be moving, perhaps sometimes able to beat the tide toward racism and sometimes being dragged along with it. So what about those people who are on the walkway but aren't doing anything? Even if they're facing away from racism, and in that sense symbolically denouncing it, they're still being moved along the track towards racism.

Dr. Ibram X. Kendi, author of *How to Be an Antiracist*, says there is no such thing as being "not racist." We are either embracing racist ideas—whether consciously or by default—*or* we are working to become more anti-racist. Even if we, as individuals, have the best intentions, as long as we're supporting racist policies and the ideas that underlie those policies, we are racist. Let that sink in for just a moment. If we aren't actively learning about and fighting against the systemic problems in our society, then we are, by default, supporting racism.

Our society, set on the foundations of a country that dehumanized Black people through slavery, has been and continues to be run largely by White men. Policies that subjugated and segregated Black people through redlining and lending practices and limited access to basic needs such as water fountains and fundamental rights like schools, ended in the mid-1900s—that was during many of our parents' lifetimes. As we've said before, change is slow.

That's why we are now at a crossroads, one where we get to make a choice about which side of history we want to be on: One that perpetuates racism and racist policies, or one that fights for a more anti-racist, equitable society, to right the wrongs of the past. It's a lot easier to stand still on that moving walkway than to turn around and stride against it. As Dr. Kendi says in his book, "Being an antiracist requires persistent self-awareness, constant self-criticism, and regular self-examination."

And part of that self-awareness is acknowledging that while of course most of us are not acting explicitly racist, as in the acts and images of racism, from subtle to harrowing, that we have been recounting, we do all have implicit biases that are largely skewed against people of color.

What can we begin to do to keep our implicit biases from rearing their heads in an ugly way?

> **MICROAGGRESSION: Questioning whether your Black neighbor owns or rents their home**

Slow down.

Time magazine's interview with Dr. Eberhardt, MacArthur Fellowship winner and author of *Biased: Uncovering the Hidden Prejudice That Shapes What We See, Think, and Do,* shared one specific example of how slowing down helped.

"I did a little informal consulting with Nextdoor.com. Most of the people go to the platform because they're trying to find a good plumber or to sell something or to alert people to various events in the neighborhood. But then there's also the 'suspicious black man' posting. Nextdoor wanted to reduce that racial profiling.

"In the tech world, they really prize being able to do everything fast, without friction. But they added friction to the platform. For the crime and safety tab, you can't just write: *There's a black man, suspicious.* You have to identify some behavior that is actually suspicious. And then be specific about what that person looks like so it doesn't sweep all black people in the same category. You know that sign, *If you see something, say something*? They changed it to, *If you see something suspicious, say something specific.* It's trying to get people to stop and think. By slowing people down, getting them to think about what they were posting, they were able to curb the profiling, they say, by about 75 percent on the site."

Slowing down allows us to check our assumptions and come up with alternative explanations for why something might be happening. We might see a speeding car and issue expletives about how selfish they are, or we can pause and consider that perhaps they were speeding to a hospital with an emergency situation in their car, and feel totally differently. We can almost always take an extra moment to employ our critical thinking skills instead of just knee-jerk responding to a fear.

Slowing down also allows us to be more altruistic and connected to our community at large. In a 1973 study on helpful behavior, forty theology students were observed on their way to give a talk on the parable of the Good Samaritan. A shabbily dressed person, clearly in need of assistance, was positioned slumped by the side of the road the seminarians used to go between two buildings. But neither the topic of their talk, nor the religious personality variables of the group, made any significant difference in predicting whether any student would stop to help the victim. The best (negative) predictor of the student helping the person was time: those students who were told that they were late to their talk—as in, those who were in a hurry—"were more likely to pass by without stopping." If we're under a tight deadline, or notice a frantic tendency in ourselves when we feel stressed out, it's helpful to be aware of the actions that time pressure—as well as mental or emotional pressures that make our thoughts and feelings spin too fast—might make us take, or might prevent us from taking. This awareness makes us better members of a community, and slowing down is good for us, too—we all know the toll that stress takes on our health and well-being.

Expand our default social circles.

We know how easy it is to be complacent about the relatively homogeneous social circles we have in this country based on our geography. The question becomes, how good is that excuse? What responsibility do each of us have to expand our real-life circles, beyond what is easy—and what difference would it make if we were to do that?

There is a body of research supporting the idea of "contact theory"—the idea that contact with an individual typically reduces one's prejudice toward a whole group, and not just the group that individual represents, but possibly other groups as well. Going outside of our immediate circle of similar friends and family opens up our minds to all sorts of other groupings of people. "Not only do attitudes toward the immediate participants usually become more favorable, but so do attitudes toward the entire outgroup, outgroup members in other situations, and even outgroups not involved in the contact."

At the very least, we can work on acknowledging people of other races. Black friends in Sara's college gospel choir said they could tell which White people had Black friends—because the ones who did would look up when they saw a Black person to search their faces to see if they were their Black friends; others simply walked by. Evidence showing that "own-race faces are better remembered when compared with memory for faces of another, less familiar race" suggests that our self-awareness and thinking about racism and anti-racism will benefit from taking the time to focus on and really see people of other races around us and learn who they are in our communities. This might start with simply saying hello to others in the grocery store aisles. It certainly means learning the names of the people you encounter regularly, whether in the workplace or during activities outside of work. It could mean asking a Black person to have coffee or take a walk, to create an opportunity to have a real conversation with someone different from ourselves. We can make these small moves towards expanding our social circles and connecting through our collective humanity.

Get into anti-racist advocacy work.

Having implicit bias is part of being human, and having those biases doesn't inherently make us bad people. Yet, we must not accept that racial inequality persists. Dr. Kendi emphasizes that "racial inequity is a problem of bad policy, not bad people." If we want to be the ones walking against the pull of the racist moving walkway we pictured a couple of pages ago, we need to put in the effort to help dismantle bad policies and replace them with those that support opportunities equally for people of all colors.

More specifically:

- Vote in your local elections with an eye towards representation of qualified BIPOC, LGBTQ+, and female candidates, because "you can't be what you can't see," and having diverse leaders helps support all of our voices.

- Look into the system of mass incarceration and see how you can help with the work being done to dismantle the mandatory minimum-sentencing requirements, reform the supermax prisons that have inhumane solitary confinement cells, and reduce the extraordinarily high prices incarcerated people and their loved ones have to pay to make phone calls to stay connected.

· Just as you might hold individuals in your lives accountable for their words, also hold the media accountable for the negative messages they send out; encourage more positive representation of Black people—and not just caricatures of the images White people have of them.

When it comes to the idea of messaging, it's good to know what works better, too. Research shows that "appeals for better conditions for African Americans stand on much firmer ground when they are bound to (and made on the basis of) better conditions for the broader society" than messages that emphasize only racism and the unfair treatment of Black Americans. Meaning, we will be more effective if we focus not always explicitly on race, racism, and discrimination, but on wanting better health care, better jobs, and better schools—things that will clearly help Black Americans and ALSO help all Americans.

Finally, take care of your own well-being while you take up the work of activism and advocacy. You alone can't save the world, and trying to do too much too quickly may soon take you out of the fight. Author and activist Mia Birdsong convincingly argues that the systems that have been pressuring Americans to do more, be more, and be perfect are ones that have been dehumanizing us as people. She says that if we reinfuse our communities with connection, humanity, and compassion, if we let ourselves slow down and connect in real life and take time to refill our own buckets, we are more likely to treat everybody with more respect. That would benefit Black and White Americans alike.

Let's work on our own humanity so we can embrace everyone's humanity, and choose to be more anti-racist for the betterment of us all.

CHAPTER 5

I Do Know Racists, Though

listen ———————————————————

The first time our White friend's mother-in-law commented about her grandson's toy, they wanted to brush it off. She couldn't *really* be racist, right?

Toddler Mike got to choose a toy at Target—and instead of a dump truck, instead of a Blonde Barbie, he chose and fell in love with a Black baby doll, whom he promptly named Baby Dylan. In the years since, Mike has apparently never been without Baby Dylan at night; Dylan goes on every trip with him.

So when Mike's grandmother asked him if his doll was *really* called Dylan, or if it was "L'Dylan," they paused. Then she asked, or, maybe, is it DeShawn, or Darius? Our friends were so shocked at what sounded like a clearly racist comment that they just said that the Black baby doll was named Dylan, and that it's not funny to joke about the doll's name like that! But the possibility of her being racist stuck in their minds.

What do you do when you know people like this? If they're provoking you, do you call them out, or do you ignore them? And what if they're sitting at your dining table over the holidays making racist jokes—do you interrupt them?

What should you do if people say or do things that are racist when, given how divided we are, it feels so painfully uncomfortable and awkward to talk about it—*especially* if you love these people?

learn ————————————————————————— 📖

The Case Against Cancel Culture

Registered dietitian and inclusive wellness advocate Dalia Kinsey hosted a conversation with Steven Wakabayashi, who'd studied meditation as he traveled the world, to discuss the latest trend of "cancel culture" (also known as "call-out culture"). You know, the thing where someone says something offensive or disagreeable and you stop following them on social media, you cancel their business contracts, you end your relationship with them in all forms.

Basically, you ostracize them from society.

If you're coming from a mindset that values punishment as a consequence for misbehavior, it sort of makes sense. You see that someone makes a mistake and you think they should pay a penalty—and that penalty is that they are erased, made insignificant in your world (which hopefully will help spread the canceling to the wider world), and that all their gains and relationships to date should be rescinded.

It's analogous, of course, to the idea of punishment for crime. Until the 1970s, rehabilitation was a focus of the U.S. prison policy. It has since become less important; state and federal governments have been incarcerating more people for longer periods of time as punishment for their actions. "[C]onsequently, the United States now has the highest rate of incarceration in the world, with a prison population growth that is 10 times greater than that of the general population; our prison population has nearly quadrupled in less than 15 years."

Our society has trended towards "erasing" from society those people who make law-breaking mistakes, by shuttling even more of them into a prison-industrial complex for longer periods of time.

Unfortunately, this methodology is not one that's sustainable for society, or good for the individuals involved. One report evaluating the system states, "If prison is viewed as a large-scale intervention, it lacks empirical support of effectiveness." Prison, the way we are using it now to isolate and punish people for a crime, does NOT work to create a safer society for us. Another study, the Stanford Prison Experiment, showed that in fact, when you put previously psychologically healthy individuals inside a prisonlike environment, they can become depressed or even sadistic in their behavior—so much so that the experiment was canceled partway through.

Outside of prisons, punishment as a method of changing behavior is likewise shown to be very ineffective. Even when it comes to helping our children mature into responsible adults, Dr. Leon Seltzer says, "corporal punishment is probably the most onerous of [these] parental options. Yet it's hardly worse than the equally shaming—and scary—'silent treatment,' which to a child is experienced as abandonment, for it involves the complete withdrawal of parental love, connection, succor, and support. In a word, it can be felt by them as a mortal threat to their parental bond."

The idea of using the silent treatment—and thus inflicting an experience of abandonment on the receiver—as a form of punishment sounds awfully similar to the idea of cancel culture. John Gottman, who has been studying relationships for years, has found that one of the biggest predictors of divorce is stonewalling—when "the listener withdraws from the interaction, shutting down and closing themselves off from the speaker because they are feeling overwhelmed or physiologically flooded."

In all of these scenarios, there is a threat of completely cutting off all communication with a person and shaking the very foundations of their sense of importance—based on, in some cases, just a single mistake. What if that person were you? Would the fear of making a mistake and being subject to cancel culture keep you from speaking out for your beliefs?

It's simply natural for human beings to be in communities. Feeling like we *matter* to our community is critical to our well-being. "Mattering" is the extent to which we make a difference in the world around us, when we feel valued and like we are adding value to others' lives. Dr. Isaac Prilleltensky states that "feeling valued is a precondition for personal health and well-being. Adding value, or making a contribution, is vital for meaning. The negative effects of not mattering, however, can be devastating. Ostracism, exclusion, and rejection are not only psychologically painful, but they can also lead to depression and aggression."

Using cancel culture as a default, blanket response to racism (or any other reprehensible behavior of someone who pushes our buttons) is an unproductive idea. Those we ostracize may in fact feel like they have to act out even more to get our attention. It's a negative spiral for everybody involved.

Just like we as a generation have shifted perspectives on how to parent—going from our own personal childhoods when parents used to pull out leather belts to spank us, to now giving our own children "natural consequences" for their actions as we talk with them about our values and choices—so too should we be looking for different ways to engage with people who do or say offensive things, so that we can remind them that we are all humans who are in it together.

The bottom line is, outright ignoring or refusing to engage with people who say or do racist things doesn't seem like the wisest choice. It says that we are defining people by their mistakes, that they're not redeemable. This stands in contrast to what we are fighting for, which is that humans should not be defined by their worst moments alone, and that intrinsically, all humans matter.

act

If canceling people who offend us and our values isn't really effective, and we want to engage them instead, what do we do?

We remember why we care.

Toddler Mike's parents are part of a generation of White parents who are working to raise their kids as anti-racist. Unfortunately, they feel like the children's grandparents are undermining them at many turns. Mike's parents buy books for their kids with Black characters, and in response the grandparents say, "Do you really think kids will see the color of the characters in the books?" Or they tell their kids that Black skin is beautiful, and the grandparents interject, "Well, *everybody* is beautiful." The family met on Zoom at the beginning of COVID, and each household in the gathering was invited to do a skit or song. The grandparents did one about "the China Flu."

Unfortunately, when Mike's parents attempt to protest, or enlighten, or request sensitivity from the grandparents, the grandparents continue to disbelieve that they are racist, pushing back with many of the responses that we commonly hear: a story about their Black friend, how poor they were growing up, denying that they've had White privilege, or invoking their old age as an excuse for them not to have to change.

When we love someone dearly, it leads to quite a bit of anxiety if they ask us, in essence, to "agree to disagree" on something so fundamental to our worldview as anti-racism.

So, back to why we care: because of the destructive power of their attitudes. If a family member or other loved one in our life can't understand someone else's perspective, if they don't have empathy toward a Black person's experience, how can we trust that they'll do what's best for our kids? What if the kids come out and that person refuses to stop referring to things as "so gay"? What if we ask them to stop praising our little girl for being skinny because we do not want to encourage body image issues, but they still won't stop commenting on her body? What if the kids befriend a person of color and that person scoffs at the friend's reluctance to wear a hoodie to go jogging? It's not about the INTENT behind the statements they're making or the things they're doing, it's about the IMPACT of them—and the impact has very real, very deep consequences.

Consider this scenario: You don't believe in Catholicism, but it's a religion that's super important to your partner, and to your partner's parents. You make what you see as a tremendous peace offering and get married in the Catholic church, and thereafter go to church repeatedly because it is a huge part of your chosen family's life. You wouldn't tell them that Jesus isn't real, you'd never berate their faith, because you understand and respect their opinions and beliefs.

By the same logic, to have someone you care about not be open to understanding why race relations and anti-racism is vitally important to you, to have them say that racism isn't real, that they don't care about how essential it is for you to raise your kids more consciously, can make you feel really disrespected.

Let's be honest: Upsetting, difficult conversations are incredibly painful to have. It's also incredibly painful to see that our loved ones don't understand how certain policies or attitudes or phrases or actions are hurting us. It can undermine our respect for them, and we *want* to respect them. The reason we want to have these conversations is because we love them and want them to continue being part of our family's lives.

We have to make decisions about how to proceed based on our own moral compass and knowledge of our own priorities and boundaries. But if we think about what is best in the longer term for our children—for Sara and Misasha, it is imperative for our kids to be raised knowing about race, racism, and how to be more anti-racist—or, for readers who aren't raising children, what is best for our communities and the people we care about, it can motivate any of us to do the difficult things in order to stand up for what is right.

Here are some points to consider.

When to Push vs. When to Stop

Of course, when someone makes a racist comment or joke, we *should* interrupt it in that moment and point it out. That's a straight statement of fact—something like, "That's a racist comment, please don't say that again." Not only does speaking up reset the assumed norm in a setting—it lets the offender know that their prejudice is NOT the norm here—but if we're in a group setting, it can also help a victim of a racist attack feel like someone has their back. Again, we are absolutely allowed to tell people that what they said was offensive to us, and to please not make jokes/use language/make bigoted remarks like that in our presence again.

Beyond that, though, we have to check in with ourselves, to see if we have the capacity to push back and lead a bigger conversation. Unless we see some indication that a person wants to listen and/or have a conversation and learn, it may be a waste of time and energy to dive in with education to try to change their beliefs. How do we gauge that?

Take a moment to think: Do we believe the person facing us is someone who is willingly racist, who does not think that Black people are as worthy as White people? OR do we think they're uninformed and haven't been in a situation where they've had to consider this before? We recommend asking questions and listening to people's responses before diving into the sort of "education" that we want to give them. Here are some ideas.

- Assuming *you're* not racist, who *is* a racist?

- Why do you think that Black people are fighting for equality?
- What is *your* ethnic and racial and religious heritage?
- If they are White: When did you realize you were White?
- What privilege do you have that others don't?

There are some basic facts you can go to to help form a foundation for a conversation about anti-racism: the history of slavery, Jim Crow laws, the truths around our nation's skewed textbooks and segregated communities and media bias. But you cannot reach someone unless they want to engage in the conversation, and if they do not, sharing information like this is usually an empty gesture, one that is unlikely to make any difference at all and ultimately only serves to make us feel better about ourselves.

That's why we think this is worth asking, even if it sounds a little woo-woo: Where is your energy? If you're feeling drained, angry, exhausted, anxious, or anything other than full of capacity to handle controversy, take a moment to consider how you want to respond. Things you say while you're feeling heated can create further division, rather than foster connected communication. And sensitive conversations like these don't often end with one pushback to a racist comment; the person on the other end is likely to reply with a counterpoint or an argument or total disagreement with what you've shared. So here's where we give permission to do something that not everybody agrees with:

Disengage.

Of course, not having a conversation that teaches a person about their racism will lead to zero change for that person. But it's important to remember that if you're not able to have a productive conversation that's helping take down biases or racist views, then it is an unproductive conversation anyway—one that won't contribute to anti-racism. These unproductive conversations will not improve the lives of Black people. They won't improve the world our kids will grow up in.

Once you feel like you've had a chance to express yourself, once you've been able to tell someone that what they said was racist—and especially if it seems like that person is just not open to hearing anything you're saying—it's okay to disengage from a conversation about race with that particular person. If they are someone you only know tangentially, perhaps you choose to disengage altogether. If they're important to you—whether a colleague at work, a close friend, or a dear family member—you can choose to set your boundaries, which we talk about below.

Engaging someone in dialogue to help them to a new understanding or feeling about a complex subject is a lengthy process, and using all your energy on one human being who can't, in that moment, see a different perspective, can destroy the stamina you need to keep going. Here are some useful actions and strategies for some of the most common situations that arise in the early stages of confronting someone about their racism (or any prejudice), including limits and boundaries you can set.

- Tell people they can't use the N-word.

- Remind them not to use a descriptor of skin color unless it's material to the story. Same goes for sexual orientation; include that detail only if it's relevant to the story.

- Maintain that they should not mock or generalize about Black names or cultural figures.

- Agree not to have conversations about race in text messages or emails; without the ability to hear tone of voice, communication can get immediately explosive. If someone texts or emails something that seems racist, simply point it out and disengage.

- When someone makes an awfully inappropriate joke, look at them deadpan and ask, "What do you mean by that?" Chances are they'll either blow you off shaking their heads, or they'll fumble as they realize that these off-color comments are in fact more hurtful and harmful than they initially thought.

- Don't engage with social media vitriol. Make one comment or statement to hold a line, but realize that back-and-forth banter is usually more harmful than helpful.

In addition to trying to constructively influence individual people, here are some other ways we can make a difference:

- Attend rallies, protests, or gatherings, if it's your style to physically show your support.

- Donate money or time to a cause that champions Black rights, and tell your family and friends, so that you may inspire them to follow suit.

- Find creative ways to use your strengths, as Brad did when he used his skills as a filmmaker to give air-time to his Black neighbors.

- Buy products from Black owned businesses (see Chapter 16, page 159, for more on this).

- Help stock your home, school, and public library with books featuring Black characters.

We encourage you to experiment with ways to make a difference. If talking to people is something that you're good at and have passion for—or even if not, but you feel it's an arena for change you can enter—develop and practice a few different scripts (in your head or on paper) for how you want to speak about your viewpoints. It's incredibly uncomfortable the first time you do or say something—be prepared for that. But decide what it is you can do, what you want to do, and commit to doing those things.

It takes all sorts of voices raised collectively to interrupt racist thoughts and patterns and actions in this country—from the privacy of our dining room tables to our larger public spheres—so even if we don't do what other people are doing, as long as we are doing something and doing it consistently, we're on this journey together.

CHAPTER 6

How Should I Talk with Black People about Race?

When's the last time something happened that made your phone blow up? Perhaps it was a happy occasion—your birthday, an anniversary, the birth of a child. Or maybe it was a stressful time, like when school districts announced that all students would be going back to remote learning and your neighborhood text chain got flooded with crying emojis.

One such time we'll never forget is the day George Floyd was murdered in the spring of 2020.

While George Floyd wasn't the first, nor will he be the last, Black man murdered at the hands of police, there were a couple of things that made this killing stand out in our collective consciousness.

The murder happened (1) the same weekend that the video of Amy Cooper, so expertly wielding White supremacy, while lying through her teeth as she called the police on a Black male bird-watcher in New York's Central Park, went viral; and (2) during the COVID shutdowns, when people's lives had already been turned upside down. So not only did Floyd's murder stand in contrast to a very clear example of White privilege, but thanks to technology, the 9 minutes and 29 seconds of the police officer kneeling on Floyd's neck while he perished was filmed and streamed across the country into all of our homes at a time when we were held captive to our screens. This became our generation's racial flashpoint moment.

listen

Most of the Black people we know tell us that their phones were buzzing and lighting up nonstop with text messages and phone calls after the video started making its rounds.

Alicia Biggs, a colleague and educator who works in the field of diversity, equity, and inclusion within public schools, who is also a Black woman, told us that after Floyd's murder, "I myself was in mourning, and was processing what probably every Black mother felt—the mourning of another one of our Black males being killed, especially in that horrific way." Given the confluence of events surrounding his death, Floyd's murder was not "just" another murder of a Black man, but one that elicited an explosion of empathy from strangers across the country.

It was reminiscent of a story that Alicia shared from her childhood. "I remember I was very young when Martin Luther King Jr. was killed. I remember my mother getting so many phone calls that day; the phone rang all day, and my mom was constantly crying. I didn't know why at the time, but I remember her sharing with us later that people from all over were calling to give their sympathy to her."

Through many moments like this, moments that will be memorialized in our history textbooks, people reach out to each other, sharing solidarity because they understand the greater impact this has both on a personal level and on a societal level. This is empathy in action.

learn

What examples can we draw on from our collective past? For many Americans, this feeling of universal mourning is similar to when the Twin Towers in New York were destroyed by terrorists in planes on Septermber 11, 2001. Or when twenty children were gunned down in their elementary school in Newtown, Connecticut, and parents reached out to each other in palpable shock and shared grief. Or, for an older generation, the day that John F. Kennedy was killed in a convertible car parading down a street in Dallas, Texas. With shattering events like these, we all remember where we were when we first heard the news, and we experienced a sense of tragedy together, knowing that the ripple effects of the awful event would be felt for a long time to come.

In the case of Black killings, unlike the tragedies of 9/11 or Sandy Hook, it seems that much more of this solidarity in mourning, anger, and hurt is felt by and directed towards Black people, while White people stand by, observing and offering sympathy from the sidelines. This difference in our reactions exposes and perpetuates the divide in our races. While George Floyd was not a national leader during his life, after his death he became a national symbol of injustice, an American citizen who got the life choked out of him as he called out for his mother, by a man paid with people's tax dollars to protect them. (We'll discuss the police further in Chapter 10, page 109.) It was an outrage and a tragedy, one that exposed the potential for police abuse and brutality to affect *any* American of *any* skin color, and yet, Misasha and Sara's phones did not blow up after his death was made public. We are not Black Americans, and so there was no outreach for solidarity in our circles. Many White Americans offered sympathy to our fellow Black Americans instead of feeling connected across races in a pivotal, tragic moment together. It's important to be aware of this pattern of "othering," because it's not new and it affects how we process events.

How does "othering" impact how we reach out to Black people about race?

We know through research that humans have empathy wired into their brains—to the point of finding that we show unconscious mimicry of people's postures, mannerisms, and facial expressions—and that humans can even be taught how to expand their empathic capacity. Having experienced the death of her father, for example, Sara empathized when one horrible day, she got news that her friend's father had passed away. She sent her friend a text message and followed up with a voicemail. She knew from personal experience how overwhelmed we can feel during such tremendous loss and grief, so she understood that her friend was operating on her own timeline of grief and reached out to her again when she hadn't heard back for a couple of weeks.

But that's how we operate for people we feel an inherent connection to. Research shows that, "[i]ndividuals tend to have the most empathy for others who look or act like them, for others who have suffered in a similar way, or for those who share a common goal." That empathy doesn't always show up as strongly when we feel we are in a different situation than someone. On top of that, as we discussed in Chapter 4, we know that implicit bias can trigger subconscious fears (see page 55). These fears can threaten our emotional stability, so it's even more important to understand that we need to put extra care into imagining and empathizing with other people's feelings when they fall into a group that is different from ours.

How does this apply to real life? Well, Alicia said that while she appreciated the calls and texts after George Floyd's murder, she also wanted to be authentic in how she responded. She needed to protect her own energy, as it felt like she had lost her own son—and she was focused on deciding how to talk with her kids about it so they had an understanding not only of the impact of this murder, but also to tie it into larger lessons about how to navigate this world as Black people. She was busy reaching out to her church members and Black organizations to see how they were processing the news individually, and how they as a community could process it together. Only then did she feel like she had the capacity to circle back to White friends who wondered how she was doing.

We asked Alicia what the response was when she finally got back to her White friends—and she let the truth fly. She was shocked and disappointed to find that friendships she thought were very solid shifted beneath her feet. Some White people acted "worse than sh*tty," assuming that since she did not answer right away, she was mad at them or no longer wanted to be their friend or acquaintance just because they were White. They had expected an immediate response, and did not have the grace to recognize that Alicia's emotions or timeline might be different than their own. Putting their concerns at the center of this exchange was a classic example of White centering.

Other White friends of Alicia's, she realized over time, either (shockingly) weren't aware that this was a tragedy worth recognizing, or were so worried about making a mistake (again, focusing on their otherness, their Whiteness), they did not reach out at all.

It was getting too exhausting, Alicia told us. She had to come to the difficult realization that if her friends couldn't prioritize other people's experiences and didn't feel that we as a society have a problem with how Black people are treated, then she could not pretend to be friends and get along. We as non-Black individuals need to continue working to take this burden off the shoulders of our Black friends and acquaintances.

For those of us relatively new to the anti-racism conversation, George Floyd's murder is probably the moment in our lifetimes we remember most clearly. However, race-based murders and crime have been happening for a long, long time—from the days of slavery to slave patrols to Jim Crow lynchings to the police brutality we see today. In 2020 alone, we can name Tyree Davis, Samuel David Mallard, Michael Rivera, Andrew Smyrna, William Howard Green Jr., Justin Lee Stackhouse, Manuel Ellis, Donnie Sanders, Lebarron Ballard, Daniel Prude, Tommie Dale McGlothen Jr., Steven Demarco Taylor, Joel Acevedo, Ahmaud Arbery, Breonna Taylor, and so many other Black people who were killed by the police. And that's not even beginning to touch on the other aggressions and microaggressions Black people face on a daily basis.

MICROAGGRESSION: Confusing one Black person for another

We can't overstate how important it is to remember that these acts of racism feel personal to many Black people. Those who are killed are not just a name in a headline or something happening to other people—this is happening to *their* in-group. They feel it personally because unlike taking off a police uniform or changing their political affiliation, they cannot change the color of their skin: It is what it is. And because these fatal acts of injustice occur on such a regular basis, it's really difficult for Black people to handle them without feeling them as assaults on who they are, their very being.

This is all to say, when you begin talking with Black people about race, please approach it very thoughtfully. Make sure you have a relationship with someone before you dive into such a personal conversation with them, and realize that this isn't some theoretical exercise—it's real, scary, and exhausting for them, and it should feel fully real to you as well. Begin the conversation respectfully and give the person you are speaking with plenty of space to respond, if and when and how they choose to. This isn't about you proving yourself as an anti-racist; this is you being a thoughtful, supportive fellow human being.

act ——————————————————————— 📢

What other options do we have to work with the insights we're gleaning here if we don't have any close Black friends?

It is very possible that you are reading this and thinking, *I don't have a relationship with a Black person close enough to talk with them about race.* As we mentioned before, there are many areas of the United States that are still segregated, where there are very few minorities, and it might feel awkward to pursue a relationship with a Black person just to pursue a relationship with a Black person.

But there are things you can do anyway.

Who are the Black people in your community? Sara's UPS delivery man, Andre, compared 2019 with post–George Floyd/COVID and said that 2020 got a little awkward. A lot of White women he delivered packages to, who previously didn't come out to chat or otherwise acknowledge him, started talking with him at many stops along his route. They'd ask him, as a Black man, if he was doing okay, and what he thought about what's happening with racism in our country. He's a pretty relaxed sort of guy, but he said he still felt awkward. How different it would have been if, over the last few years, his customers had already been walking outside to chat with him—about the weather, what it's like working at UPS, his life, their life, and oh my goodness, how are the kids doing during COVID?

If you look to establish a baseline of connection now with those you might simply be brushing shoulders with—remembering again that this isn't about rushing into things but committing to longer-term change—then perhaps over time, you will have the type of relationship where you *can* begin asking questions about topics like race and racism.

Keep in mind that, just like we as White people aren't expected to be the authority on all White people, **Black people should not be expected to be the authority on all Black people.** Our friend Brandon commented once that he gets frustrated when people ask him what he thinks about a Black person who committed a crime, as in, doesn't he think it "makes all Black people look bad"? As we've said before, our human tendency to put people into similar buckets can be quite powerful, and Brandon rightfully refuses to feel any sort of responsibility for another person's actions just because they have similar skin color. He pointed out that it's like saying, "Well, you're White, you're responsible for Hitler and the Unabomber and the guy who shot up Sandy Hook." Seems horribly outrageous, right? We can't hold people responsible for the actions of others in their race.

Similarly, Black people are not responsible for being our teachers about racism. You can ask people how they individually feel about how they've been treated, but you should plan to learn about racism and how to be more anti-racist *outside* of your individual relationships with Black people too.

MICROAGGRESSION: Assuming that one person speaks for all people of that same group

Beyond developing relationships with individuals you come across regularly, **look for opportunities to practice and develop empathy.** Go to Black history and Native American history museums, to museums exhibiting the remnants of the internment camps. Watch TV shows that feature characters of color, and practice listening to other people's stories without triggering your own defensiveness. Volunteer at organizations that serve people in need so you can provide support for others who live in your community.

Look for spaces where you can have conversations about race. Book clubs are a fantastic place to start; there are many, many books—both fiction and non-fiction—that offer intelligent, in-depth, and various perspectives on race, and include questions to discuss. If you prefer having a more guided book club, you can approach your local library to help you connect with other people who want to focus on reading and discussing books specifically about race issues; or you can find out which of your neighbors, coworkers, or fellow parents might be interested in starting a book club, and perhaps agree to hire a facilitator to lead these difficult conversations. For some of our favorite book club books, see the Recommendations section on page 225.

We've also seen groups formed to take it upon themselves to begin learning about anti-racism. At your workplace, for example, you could ask to create a webinar series on a quarterly basis with the purpose of talking about race. Consider asking your pastor or religious leader to create a group discussing racism within your spiritual community. While some people may be resistant, standing up to ask for conversation within these communities might be just the drop in the pond that begins a ripple effect of change.

CHAPTER 7

And Is It "Black" or "African American"?

listen

Sara was talking with a mom friend on her porch about someone we didn't yet know well when her friend's voice suddenly dropped mid-sentence. Sara could barely catch what she was saying. Turns out she was saying, "You know, the Black family"—as if she was talking about something shameful and someone might be around to hear her. Then she got flustered and said, "I never know how to refer to people of color, is it always 'African American,' or is it okay to say 'Black'?"

Great question. Why is the distinction between the descriptions "Black" and "African American" important? Because they're speaking for fundamental differences between people who share the same skin color.

learn

Black people have lived a history of being called different things. You'll read more about the origins of the N-word in Chapter 9 (page 101), and you'll hear in no uncertain terms that it is a word White people should never use. But there have been many other words—acceptable and not—that have been used over the years to describe people with Black skin.

In the 1800s, "colored" started gaining popularity because it included people with full African heritage as well as those who were mixed race. (It's no longer an acceptable term, as along with other reasons, it's reminiscent of the Jim Crow–era discrimination.)

In 1850, the government asked their census enumerators to record Black people, mulattos (someone who is Black and at least one other race), Black slaves, and mulatto slaves separately. (The word "mulatto" is usually offensive today.)

For the census in 1890, there was interest in quantifying mixed-race people, as the government added categories that included "quadroon" (one-fourth "black blood") and "octoroon" (one-eighth or less of "black blood").

While quadroon, and octoroon were quickly dropped for the 1900 census, mulatto was restored as a category in 1910.

By the 1930 count, the mulatto category was dropped, but this census formalized the "one-drop" rule: census enumerators were instructed that "a person of mixed White and Negro blood was to be categorized as Negro, no matter how small the percentage of Negro blood." (Nope, Negro is not a word to be used anymore either.)

By the twentieth century, many Black Americans had started rejecting the labels "Negro" and "mulatto" and "colored." In the 1960s, leaders in the Black Power movement, including Malcolm X, moved to be called "Black."

MICROAGGRESSION: Telling a person, "You're not *really* Black/Hispanic/Asian/Indigenous/etc"

Then, in 1988, the term "African American" became popular in the United States thanks to a strong push in a speech by Reverend Jesse Jackson, who wanted to move the ethnonym (the name applied to an ethnic group) away from purely a racial, or physical, association and closer to a more ethnic, or cultural and geographic, association. Since many Black people in the United States then were as now descendants of slaves who were taken from Africa, it seemed like a fitting name.

But African American is a heavier phrase for Black people who descend from slavery. Consider this story. Misasha's young sons were asked to do a family tree for their second-grade social studies class. You know, the ones where you ask each of your parents where their families are from, and you color in the map and draw the appropriate flag near those countries. The boys were able to color in a Scottish flag and a Japanese flag for their mom. When they went to ask their father, however, the history of slavery reared its very real head. Misasha's husband's family was brought to the United States as slaves, and they have no record of which country they were from. All the boys could do was say that they did not know where their father's family was from because of slavery. Misasha had to have an awkward discussion with the teacher to prepare her for the likelihood that other parents might not be ready for their kids to come home discussing slavery based on a family history project. (To her credit, the teacher was open and receptive to this question, and she and Misasha were able to turn what was uncomfortable into something that felt good—simply by listening, and understanding).

So here we are: Black and African American are the two main terms we use to describe Black people in our mainstream vernacular today. Let's look again at why is it important to differentiate.

During the 1990s, more than half a million Africans immigrated to the United States—more than had come in the 150 years before. This nearly tripled the number of Black people in the United States with recent ancestry in sub-Saharan Africa. This gave the term "African American" a whole new meaning, because it identified both those with anonymous ancestral ties to Africa through slavery, as well as those who identified as part African through recent lineage, like President Barack Obama, whose father was from Kenya.

At the same time as the increase in immigration from Africa, there was a 60 percent increase in Black people with origins in the Caribbean coming to the United States. This meant that there was also a huge increase in Black people living in the U.S. who were NOT from Africa, who were from or descended from a multitude of different island nations. Vice President Kamala Harris's father was born and raised in Jamaica and immigrated to the United States as an adult, for example. Yet their skin color looks the same as those from Africa.

This rich mix of heritage points to the importance of getting to know people's stories, and reminds us that we cannot see a Black person in our travels throughout our days, from street to stores to meetings to our children's school classrooms, and guess at that person's experience based solely on their appearance.

act ———————————————————————— 📢

So what should I call people with "black" skin if I don't know them?

In general, if you don't know specifically, it's acceptable to default to Black—because you don't yet know where their families descend from. But the nuanced answer is, it depends on who you ask. Alicia Biggs, the Black educator who shared her experience around George Floyd's murder in Chapter 6 (see page 72), tells us that she uses the term "African American" in a professional or educational setting if the person's heritage is not clear. When she's with her friends or her children, she code-switches and uses "Black." Some people have very strong views on what they want to be called; we encourage people to define what groups they belong to and tell us what they want to be called. It reminds us of the gender identity conversations about pronouns—if a person wants to be called they/them, then that's what we call them. When people tell us they want to be called either Black or African American, that's what we call them.

It's up to us to listen first, ask if necessary, and get to know the person, so we can use their terminology in our conversations.

What do we do about older people who still use inappropriate labels?

We have heard from both Black and White people alike that their grandparents still use outdated terms like "colored." Recognizing that those were the terms used when they were growing up, our generation can choose to gently correct them by responding with the correct term, like "oh Granddad, you mean that Black woman over there?"

We are all ignorant until we learn; we will all make mistakes. And once you learn, there's no imperative for you to go back and apologize. It's a lot more graceful to thank someone for teaching you, and to remember their preferences for future encounters.

CHAPTER 8

How Do I Make Sure I Teach My Kids Well?

listen ———————————————

One day, long, long ago, Sara's three-year-old daughter was sitting at her little wooden kiddie table immersed in coloring. Sara was puttering around the kitchen when her daughter asked, "Mama, can I have the skin-color crayon?" Sara's bustle came to a screeching halt—for whatever reason, she recognized that this was an important moment.

Sara hadn't yet had any substantial background in race-based conversations—hadn't yet consciously considered buying books with diverse characters in them, certainly didn't know that kids can identify racial differences from the time they're six months old. She just knew she didn't quite understand what her kiddo was asking, or what the child herself understood, and she needed to talk about it.

"What is the skin color you're looking for, baby?" Sara asked as she walked over to her. Rolling up her sleeve, Sara squatted and put her arm right next to daughter's pudgy little bare arm, and started babbling, "Because look, you and I have different color skin—it looks sort of similar, but if you look closely, I'm a little less pink than you are. And you know there are so many different colors of skin, so many shades of brown, light and dark, and we think all of the skin colors are beautiful! So, when you say skin-color crayon, what color is that, how would you name your skin?"

Sara was rambling through an unplanned monologue but knew she had landed on a good question, because her daughter lit up and said, "I have peach skin, mama, so I want the peach-color crayon!" And just like that, the moment was over.

learn

Kids understand race—and they understand it when they're young.

Science has come a long way, and we have been able to learn that children understand race from a very young age.

Thanks to technology, scientists can use the visual preference paradigm to study visual discrimination in infants. In practical terms, what does that mean? They record eye movements, and independent observers analyze the film frame by frame by on a computer using specialized software. They deduce that the thing being watched the most is the preferred thing.

Through this, they've found that at birth, babies look equally at faces of all races, but by the time they're three months old, babies look more at faces that match the race of their caregivers. By the time children are three to five years old (even if they're in ethnically diverse day care centers, as children don't just learn from their caregivers but also take in a lot from their surrounding communities), they use racial categories to identify themselves, and include/exclude children from activities. In fact, Katz and Kofkin showed that by thirty months—that's just shy of three years old—most children use race to choose playmates. Specifically, at that age, most children (over 65 percent) demonstrated that they preferred to play with people of their same race.

Here's where it gets really shocking, though. In the study, these preferences began to shift at just around thirty months old, and by thirty-six months, the number of White children who wanted to play with kids of their same race increased from 65 percent to 82 percent, while the number of Black children who wanted to play with their same race decreased to 32 percent—meaning that the majority of *both* Black and White children chose to play with White children.

That made our jaws drop.

We had already been immersed in studying the research and observing in our own lives that people like people who are similar to them, as we've been sharing in this book so far, so why on earth would this research show that Black children as well as White choose to play with White children?

One fairly simple explanation is that Black children may have more exposure to different races than White children have. When we look at the numbers of people with homogenous social circles, Black families are less likely to have solely Black friends, and so even at a very young age, their children may follow this model at school.

A more troubling explanation is that the different numbers are a reflection of society's messages about race, including the messages that we, as parents share—or don't. Scientists say that parents in general are more willing to talk about most groupings of people, like gender, for example, than race.

Looking back, even looking back at just last week, we can't tell you how many times we have said, "Oh, what a good girl!" or "Atta boy!" or even "Girls can do anything!" Gender words are all around us. Pronouns, stereotypes . . . we play into them all, from the time the children are very little.

Can you see yourself in this?

As a society, we also often address differences in physical characteristics outside of skin color. We describe the kid at the playground as taller, or shorter, than our kid. We talk about how strong someone is for kicking the soccer ball the length of the field, or how much faster they are able to run. We talk about the blond kid, the brunette kid. Sara even remembers her kids asking a woman in a wheelchair in the Target bathroom what it was for, and she replied that sometimes people need help moving around. Just stating a fact and moving on.

We even talk more openly about age difference than skin color. Years ago, Sara's toddler was sitting on the Home Depot paint counter waiting for the paint mixer to be done, when an old woman walked up to the counter next to them. In typical shameless toddler fashion, her child stared at this woman's deeply wrinkled face and then pivoted her head towards Sara. "Mom, why does her face look like that?" Sara knew she had a choice: Speak clearly or crumble. It was embarrassing, but since we do talk about "when you grow up" or how "we respect our elders," Sara told her that people's skin changes as they get older.

People are DIFFERENT. We each have our own set of characteristics. So do we bring the same level of candor that we do about gender, age, height, hair color, and even abilities to conversations about human variations in skin tone?

Not many of us do. According to the same paper by Katz and Kofkin cited earlier, fewer than one-fourth of the parents—irrespective of racial group—commented on racial differences they saw in real life like at the playground or in stores, or on TV.

For some reason, we don't want to call attention to differences in race.

Have you ever experienced that super-awkward moment when somebody is trying to point someone out across the park, struggling to come up with ways to describe that person without mentioning their race? Say it's a group of kids on bikes and they're like, no, no the kid with the socks with that little blue stripe up the leg. And you're squinting trying to figure out which kid that is, until you realize it's the one Black kid in a group of White kids. Saying that would have made it really easy to understand who they were talking about, but they don't, because that would be calling attention to racial difference.

It's like we've been conditioned *not* to talk about it.

But if we're not talking about race, if we are avoiding conversations about race, it "sends a message that there's something off-limits, and even bad, about racial differences," wrote Dr. Wanjiku Njoroge, a board-certified child psychiatrist and adjunct professor of psychiatry at Yale whose research focuses on the impact of culture on early infant and childhood development. The truth is, kids are forming ideas about race regardless of whether we talk about it, and as parents, we cannot delude ourselves about that. And by the time White children are about five, most of them attribute negative characteristics to Black people and positive characteristics to White people. Read that again, please, because it surprised us too. **By the time children are FIVE YEARS OLD, they have racial bias.**

Where are they getting the messages from, and what sort of messages are they? (And importantly: Are we okay with the messages they're getting?) As stated above, while only one-fourth of people surveyed had open conversations about race, Black adults are more likely to say that race or race relations come up *often* in conversation with family and friends (27 percent), compared with White (11 percent), Hispanic (15 percent), and Asian (13 percent) adults. As the segment of the population that bears the brunt of racism in the United States, it has become more normalized for Black people to engage regularly in these conversations. As White people, we can also choose to normalize conversations about race and racism in our circles so we nurture awareness and are the source of the messages our children get.

Additionally, while many of us know this to various degrees and have thought about it a little or a lot, there is more and more indisputable data about the importance of representation in the media—or lack thereof—that helps form children's understanding about race. Television portrayals, positive or negative, greatly influence viewers' stereotypes of Black Americans; and when we don't have Black people in our real life to compare these stereotypes to, television images have a huge effect on viewers' perceptions.

How has the media portrayed Black people? Drawing on data from decades past, Black people on TV typically have had lower status roles and lower educational levels than White people. Black people have generally been depicted in blue collar or service occupations like postal worker or house cleaner, or in occupational roles like a servant, entertainer, musician, athlete, or cook. In one of the earliest studies on this topic, the U.S. Commission on Civil Rights (1977) found that "African American television portrayals typically depicted the following stereotypic personality characteristics: inferior, stupid, comical, immoral, and dishonest. Researcher [Jannette] Dates (1990) later noted that other stereotypes of African Americans existed, including disrespectful, violent, greedy, ignorant, and power-driven."

Have you noticed any of these trends? What do you see when you cast a more critical eye on the shows that you and your family watch? Do you see many people of color in main speaking roles? What stereotypes do they embody?

While representation has been increasing and role types have been reflecting more positive attributes over the last decade, the media that we are exposed to—and that our children are exposed to—are not only *not* accurate representations of the breadth of the Black population, but are distorting our image of who Black Americans actually are. Considering the paucity of Black television station owners and producers and journalists and experts, White people are defining what Blackness is for the rest of the country— and those stereotypes of Blackness haven't been the most accurate or positive.

We'll come back to television and movies in that pages that follow, where we talk about some of the many ways available to parents for teaching their kids about diversity of race and other cultures.

act ──────────────────────────────────────

So as parents, how should we expose our kids to race?

It can sometimes feel overwhelming to consider how to have explicit conversations with our children about things that we ourselves have had the privilege to avoid for a large part of our lives. But talking about race doesn't have to be terrifying; there are easier entry points now more than ever before.

Acknowledge Whiteness.

By not talking about race explicitly with our White kids, our kids are very likely to assume that theirs is the default race against which all other races should be judged. That *they* are the normal ones, and all others are different. You may have heard the phrase "centering Whiteness"—we don't want to do that. As the Conscious Kid points out, "It is important to name whiteness and for White people to identify as 'White.' Not naming or claiming the word 'White' masks whiteness, white supremacy, and white privilege, power, and history as members of the dominant racial group."

If talking about race is fairly new to you, especially if you're White, it's important that you explore your *own* racial identity as a White person before discussing race with your children.

Before you dive into the race conversation with your kid, we suggest you ask yourself the following questions—and answer them honestly. It's a good idea to grab a journal or notebook to write down your answers, so you can look back and see how your thinking evolves over time and where you can better focus your energy:

- How comfortable are you talking about race?

- How do you react when confronted with racist behavior?

- In what ways have you ignored this behavior in the past?

- Why is it important for everyone to work towards ending injustice?

For a longer, more thorough list, download our free PDF journal with the prompts at dearwhitewomen.com.

Once you've given these questions some thought—and we know, as you should, that your answers are subject to change as you learn more—you can begin inviting your children into the conversation. Raising race-conscious, anti-racist children will be part of the long-term solution to the divide that is splitting our country.

Show them more Black main characters.

Books are a natural and wonderful way to expose our children to the world. Kids love books, even if you have to search for the ones that capture their fancy. And you may need to dig a little to find books that communicate kid-sized concepts of diversity and race issues, just as you may have to dig a little to find books that normalize Black characters beyond their race. Research as recent as 2018 shows that more than half of all reviewed children's books featured White children, and that books featuring animals and other nonhuman characters were reviewed more than all types of visible minorities combined. According to the Cooperative Children's Book Center, "taken together, books about White children, talking bears, trucks, monsters, potatoes, etc. represent nearly three-quarters (71 percent) of children's and young adult books published in 2019." Our children are reading more stories with talking animals than characters who look Black or Brown!

If you like to read—which, evidenced by the fact that you have this book in your hands right now, you probably do—then you probably read to your kids, too. Books are a win-win means for addressing the representation gap in your own home. Go to the library and get books with more diverse characters. "[Y]ou can introduce race through books and through play," suggests the renowned psychiatrist Njoroge. "Talk about how there are different genders, different races, languages, and cultures. Tie their questions to education—get out the globe or the map and tell stories." The stories we read to our children can be used as springboards for having our own conversations with them. Not a one-and-done race conversation, but rather conversations that encourage critical thinking, interject our own view about accepting and respecting difference, and let our children know that we are open to talking about race. There are incredible resources out there to help us find these books, including the Conscious Kid and, of course, our list of our favorites (see Recommendations, page 225).

Another fix for the vacuum of Black role models in mainstream media is to start paying close attention on that front to the TV and movies that you are letting your children watch. We tend to censor from our homes shows that depict violence; why not censor shows that feature all-White casts? Media is starting to trend in a more conscious direction, and producers respond well to pressure by what is being watched, so don't let them get complacent by giving them the advertising dollars for watching nondiverse shows. Turn on *Doc McStuffins*, turn on *The Amazing Race*—even turn on the Barbie movies that are increasingly offering diverse storylines.

MICROAGGRESSION: Saying, "she's pretty, for a Black girl"

Now that issues about representation are so much clearer, Sara has encouraged her family to watch shows like *Mixed-ish* or *Black-ish*, to expose everyone to a range of race and culture narratives while taking in some easy entertainment. At first, it felt awkward and contrived to put on a show talking about and featuring people of color, like she was trying to make a point about race. (Can you relate?) She felt like they were intruding into "other" people's territory. And yet, these shows gave her family a glimpse into how it might feel to be a Black family, who, just like the rest of us, are largely exposed to media that feature White people and their cultural norms.

For this reason, in Misasha's house, shows that feature Black families are really all the family watches. Since portrayals of White people in the media are easy to come by, they make the extra effort to make sure their children see themselves represented in the media they take in. And they always cheer when HGTV features a non-White family in its home remodels or house hunting—because it's that rare.

One last shout-out: Considering the huge preponderance of White representation in American media entertainment, it's obvious why the movie *Black Panther* was such a tremendous film for Black Americans. It has a cast of all Black people, heroic and strong and not in need of any rescuing by White people. Misasha shares that her husband—who isn't the kind of guy who goes to movies on opening night, and isn't the kind of father who shows PG-13 rated movies to their young children—made a point of taking their older son to see *Black Panther* on opening night. It was that important to them to be able to show their sons images of powerful, inspirational people in their own likenesses.

Be conscious about your—and your kids'—social circles.

As Debra Van Arsdale states in her piece from 1996, "Young children's ability to manage and understand the social world is not nearly as limited as mainstream theories of development would have us believe. . . . Children have social experiences first, and then incorporate those experiences into an overall personal framework of social action. . . . For most children, the racial-ethnic issues arise forcefully within the context of interaction with other children."

Children learn through their reality, not just by people *telling* them things about the world. This country has many pockets of segregation, and without a conscious effort, children might grow up not really knowing children of other ethnicities. But as you can imagine, telling kids that we are nice to Black people is very different than being nice to the Black friend who comes over for dinner. That personal connection—those first social experiences that allow them to develop their own personal framework of society—is a very powerful force.

What can I do to foster friendships across color lines, for myself and for my children?

Sometimes it feels like we don't have any contacts across the race spectrum. One of the Black moms in our kids' school shared that she did everything that the White moms do, from being a smiling, happy class mom to volunteering with the PTA to heading up the Girl Scout troop—but she was never invited to join a book club or happy hour with the other moms. Are there people like this who are around, but aren't invited? If so, invite them!

There is no pressure to make friends with people simply *because of* their race. We have spoken with Black moms in predominantly White areas who jumped on friendships with other Black families just because they wanted to create solidarity for their children. But the kids' personalities didn't jibe and they realized they were forcing something just for the sake of race, which we don't recommend. Take an honest look around. School, work, religious groups, neighborhoods, your local YMCA—especially when the kiddos are little, these environments offer great opportunities to get to know other parents and develop cross-cultural relationships. Developing connections is the tie that binds communities, whether people jibe personally or not, and creates the chance for friendships to form when they do.

One really effective way to integrate diversity into your daily life is by way of your essential-needs roster and the people we go to for quality-of-life priorities. Find out if there is a Black pediatrician or dentist in your network that you can take your child to. If there is a Black librarian in your area, make theirs your go-to library. Request that your child be assigned to the class with a Black teacher, and seek out Black instructors for extra-curricular activities like swimming, dance, or crafting classes. We've said it before: We acknowledge that coordinating all these efforts can be a difficult proposition. But you never know how that might change the trajectory of your family's life.

And keep talking about race.

White people are in fact part of the spectrum of skin color—and not outside of it. We need to point this out to our children and start to have fact-based conversations about race when they're little.

When they're young, teach your kids that the way we currently think about race is something that people and societies have invented; it grew out of a need for people to define people based on how they look. That concept of race has us believing that the human species is clearly divided into distinct groups on the basis of inherited physical and behavioral differences—but that isn't really true. White, Black, and Brown skin colors exist along the entire spectrum, and we all have our own unique shades.

As the kids get older, we can start talking about what happens *because* of race.

Racism is defined as a "prejudice, discrimination, or antagonism directed against a person or people on the basis of their membership in a particular racial or ethnic group, typically one that is a minority or marginalized." It's basically something that creates the hierarchy and advantages for those people in the majority (White privilege) through things like laws, institutions, policies, and even just cultural messages.

A simple way of defining racism is "prejudice plus power," but there are different types of racism, including individual, systemic, and institutional. There's a lot packed into it. How do we explain that to kids? If you're looking for a script, you can say something like, "You know how there are so many different types of people, different races who have different shades of skin? Well, because our country was founded with slave labor, where White people controlled Black bodies to make money, there are all sorts of lingering things in our society that mean that Black people are *still* treated worse than White people are. That's called racism."

So here's the $1 million question. Why should we be taking this on with our children now, especially when everything around race feels so uncomfortable?

In addition to the moral pull of humanity and desire for harmony, we believe our children will be much better prepared for their future and their *own* children's futures if we make the decision to stand on this side of history. White kids are projected to become a minority in the United States around the year 2045; the census data shows White people dropping below 50 percent of the population within our children's lifetime. In fact, by 2020 (although as of this writing, the census data is still being tabulated), less than half of children in the United States are projected to be non-Hispanic White alone (49.8 percent of the projected 74.0 million children under age 18). The percentage of people talking about race, racism, and anti-racism in their lives is likely to increase, and we want to give our children an advantage by giving them the tools to participate in the critical conversations that will be the basis for a stronger, more united nation.

How will we know if our efforts with our kids have made a difference?

As Sara was taking a break from writing this particular chapter today to have lunch with one of her kiddos, something happened. Her elementary school–aged child said something racist.

They were talking about a video her daughter was watching for school, and—presumably because the child knows how much conversations about race matter to Sara—her daughter was pointing out that this platform featured Black adults and Black kids. She continued, "And yeah, the girl in this video is Black, and she's still pretty!"

THEN, before Sara could even open her mouth to take a breath, her daughter caught what she herself had said.

"Oh, no, Mom, I said something racist!" she exclaimed, at which point Sara's jaw dropped a little, and then her daughter said, "I should have just said, she's Black, *and* she's pretty!"

As of this writing, Sara's daughter is nine years old. This is the same little girl who sat at the coloring table asking for the skin-color crayon when she was three. They've been talking about race, racism, and being anti-racist for about two-thirds of her life, and even though she is still in elementary school, even though she presents as White, she caught herself saying something so tiny (and yet so huge)—something that many adults wouldn't have thought twice about it.

We can't promise perfection when raising kiddos with this anti-racist lens held as steadily as possible in the center of a busy family's life, but we do know that children who bring awareness to their own actions, who know how to question a narrative with a broader mind, and then share that perspective with others—even if it's one conversation at a time—can change the world. It is worth the effort.

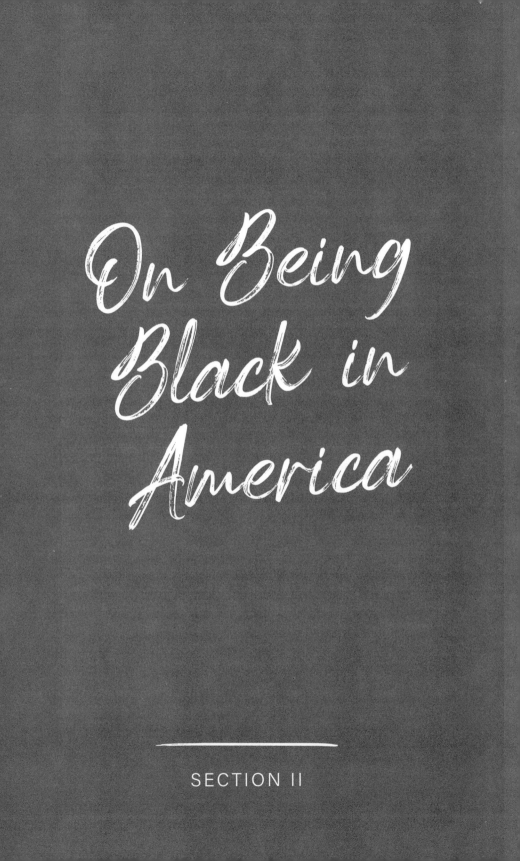

On Being Black in America

SECTION II

CHAPTER 9

Isn't the N-Word Okay Sometimes?

During the time we were writing this book, a White conservative female judge named Amy Coney Barrett was confirmed to the Supreme Court. If you remember that process, the N-word took center stage as Justice Barrett defended (and later, it was discovered, misrepresented) her finding that the use of the N-word alone does not necessarily constitute a hostile work environment. In other words, a man could be called the N-word and the use of that word alone doesn't mean that he's in an unfriendly or hostile space.

Screech.

If you listened very closely at that moment, you probably heard the sound of every Black person's collective jaw drop on the ground—along with a huge number of non-Black peoples'. And then you could feel the collective eye roll. To us, the wrongness of this was a no-brainer. To Misasha's Black husband, it seemed laughable—yet not surprising. He's intimately familiar with how White people misunderstand the power of the N-word and the hate that comes along with it.

But what wasn't surprising to any of us was the number of well-intentioned White people who immediately sprang to Justice Barrett's defense, saying in not so many words, what was the big deal about the N-word anyway? It's just a word. Black people use that word, they point out (or as one commenter on Facebook insisted as she challenged our representation of the N-word as a hard stop when it comes to a hostile work environment: Don't "the brothers" use that word to refer to each other?). If Black people can use that word, then it can't be all that bad, right?

Wrong. Very, very wrong.

We're here to remind you not just that the N-word alone is sufficient to create a hostile environment in most people's minds, but that every Black person who has been called the N-word in their lifetime that we have spoken with has a distinct formative memory of the moment when they were first called that name, who said it, and who came to their defense. More often than not, the first time was when they were kids, the perpetrator was a White person— sometimes a White mom—using that word to refer to them in a way that definitely invoked hatred and pain . . . and no one came to their defense.

If you don't think that's scarring, then you haven't listened to enough Black people tell their stories.

If you don't think that creates a searing, burning pain, then you don't have kids who you look at and know that one day it will happen to them, and it tears at your heart because you can't stop it from happening.

If you don't think that immediately creates a distinct loss of self-worth, then that word has never been directed at you.

listen ———————————————————

Maybe hearing these stories will help.

One day Antonio, a young boy about seven years old, was walking home from elementary school with a White girl his age who lived close by. Along their walk home, a stranger opened the front door of their house, came out, and screamed at the girl: "Hey, you don't need to be walking with that [N-word]! You come here right now!" His friend reluctantly went over to talk to the angry person.

Antonio had no idea what was going on; he knew this friend well, and wasn't sure if he should call the police or run to a house with an orange sticker indicating it was a "safe place" for elementary school kids. He thought the person yelling from the house might be trying to abduct his friend. He froze and waited. The girl came back, and when he asked what happened, she said, "Yeah, that person's racist, she told me I shouldn't be walking with you because you're a Black person."

Little seven-year-old Antonio told his mom what had happened, and they had to sit down to have a more serious talk, including what the N-word means. He realized in that moment that life wasn't what was portrayed on Sesame Street—that it's much bigger and scarier than that.

If you are a person who doesn't think this word is a big deal, read on. We're about to unpack some of the history around the creation and use of the N-word that should make you think twice about *ever* using that word or allowing anyone around you to use that word without telling them exactly why it is highly racist.

learn ————————————————————

Let's start with the meaning behind the word. Because if you're like us, you may not have thought about how certain words—and their meanings—change throughout history. The N-word is no exception.

According to the *Merriam-Webster's Dictionary*, the very first known use of the N-word was in 1574, when it was used as an "insulting and contemptuous term for a Black person." It is believed that the word is an alteration of the word "Black" in many other languages (in Middle French, *negre*; in Spanish or Portuguese, *negro*; in Latin, *niger*). Several accounts of the first slaves being brought from Africa to the New World in 1619 theorize that the word "niger" was used to refer to the color of these slaves' skin. (Clearly humans were making judgments about skin color well before America was officially "founded"!) The Portuguese and Spanish slave traders reportedly used this word in a patronizing way, and likely with some mild racism, but it seems without the overt hate that the use of the word came to carry over time.

Since that point, however, with the entrenchment of slavery in our country as a way to get free labor and the simultaneous reinforcement of the fact that as long as there was slavery there would be people who were locked into providing said free labor, the word took on usage and meanings separate from simply the color of someone's skin. Merriam-Webster provides three defini-tions for this word, all of which start with the label "offensive," and all of which relate to someone's *worth* as defined by the color of their skin.

Some people believe the current dictionary definitions defining the N-word as a hateful, racist epithet is a recent change and that the original meaning was "an ignorant person"—that is, a Black person, since Black people weren't allowed to go to school and there-fore weren't "smart" in the White American sense. That argument suggests that the word did not have the racist or hateful meaning that it does now. It is important to note that this is not accu-rate. Merriam-Webster points out that the first time the N-word appeared in one of its dictionaries was 1864, "at which time it was defined as a synonym of *Negro*, with a note indicating that it was used 'in derision or depreciation.'" **There's never been an alternate, more palatable definition for this word in the dictionary.**

In fact, we know through first-person accounts from the 1800s that the N-word was already being directed at Black people to make them feel inferior and to reinforce impressions of their sub-human nature—thereby deepening the earlier patronizing tone to one of hate and racism. Some theorize that this use of the N-word was due to the rise in the number of free Black people in the United States, and the resulting threat that White people felt when society as they knew it was changing, perhaps in ways that they did not like or understand.

We also know from this same time period that slave owners used the N-word to refer to slaves. As one writer points out, slave owners often categorized slaves as "salt-water" if recently brought over, or "country-born" for those slaves born in America. The word that always followed those categorizations, however, was the N-word (movies like *Twelve Years a Slave* dramatize vividly how hurtful and charged this word can be in that context).

This brief history of the spread of the N-word provides us with food for thought about who also came to use the word. It was what the slaves heard, without fail, in reference to themselves and other slaves, and so it was that word that they then took up to refer to each other. Because many of the slaves were African, the hard *er* ending of the N-word, almost unpronounceable in most African dialects, was replaced with the easier to pronounce, softer, open vowel sound *ah*, and the term gained some power for the slaves using it themselves, as it reinforced that they were "survivors and humans whose freedom and dignity had been assaulted."

Thus, even though the origin of the word in that context was largely the same—the use and meaning were not. **When used by White people or non-Black people, the N-word was a term of hate and violence; when used by some Black people to refer to each other, it was a symbol of resistance.**

"It's impossible to separate the word from various manifestations of White supremacy," said Jabari Asim, an Emerson College literature professor and author of *The N Word: Who Can Say It, Who Shouldn't, and Why.* "Racist violence against Black people has seldom been implemented without the recitation of the N-word at the same time."

That said, it's disconcerting to learn how easily, and how completely, the N-word worked itself into "polite" White society as a result. Are you familiar with the nursery rhyme that starts "Eeny, meeny, miny mo?" Well, you might be surprised as to what that original rhyme was. Ready?

> *Eeny, meeny, miny, mo.*
> *Catch a nigger by his toe.*
> *If he hollers, let him go.*
> *Eeny, meeny, miny, mo.*

Yeah.

The N-word was common not only in kids' nursery rhymes, but also coming out of the mouths of people who were in charge. Supreme Court Justice James Clark McReynolds referred to Howard University as the "nigger university." President Harry S. Truman called Congressman Adam Clayton Powell "that damned nigger preacher." "Nigger" was also in the vocabulary of Senator, Vice President, and President Lyndon Baines Johnson. "I talk everything over with [my wife]," he proclaimed on one occasion early in his political career. Continuing, he quipped, "Of course . . . I have a nigger maid, and I talk my problems over with her, too."

When presidents and Supreme Court justices can just slip the N-word into casual conversation and jokes, you know that it was more commonplace than we would like to believe. And, as you can tell from the varied usages of the term, it was designed to be derogatory, disparaging, hurtful, and violent. It was designed to keep a whole race of people "in their place."

So why is it important to know the history of the N-word? Because when we don't know the history behind the word, we don't understand its power. And we can't ignore this important point. As noted by Teaching Tolerance, "[r]apper Common, in his preface to the February 2014 ESPN 'Special Report on the N-Word,' offers this historical connection and disconnect among those who do not know what needs to be known, understood, and passed along: The N-word is a euphemism to shield us from the shame of our past. . . . It is a polite code for the slur, but the slur itself—*Nigger*—that looks like a Sunday morning in Alabama when five Black girls went into the bathroom of their church, and only one came out."

The power of the word, and the violence and hate behind that word, cannot be understated.

act

Where do we go from here? Well, there are many ways to address the power and hate in this word in our own small spheres of power. First off (and this may seem simple, but it can get obscured at times): **For those of us who are not Black, the N-word should never come out of our mouths, and it's important that we tell this to our children.** Not even if we are at karaoke and someone puts on Kanye's "Golddigger" (the explicit version)—we don't say that word.

We must recognize that, not being Black, we don't appreciate and understand the nuances with which Black people choose—or actively choose against—using this word. But the key learning here is that other peoples' usage of the word isn't our decision, and the fact that some Black people use the N-word should never be used by a non-Black person as a way to justify their own use of it. Unavoidably, using the word as a non-Black person invokes the hate and violence that caused over four thousand Black people to be lynched in the South. It carries the hate and violence of domestic terrorism. We cannot be complicit in that.

Whether or not Black people choose to use the N-word to stand for their strength and resilience; whether they use it to take back the power from the word and change it from hurt to love; or whether they choose to reject it entirely, due to its racist and violent history—that is their choice, not ours. **When words have power in their impact, it is the impacted group that gets to choose how that word is used by them—and only them.** Our opinion there doesn't matter, and their choice with regard to how they use the word shouldn't impact our ban on using the word.

Obviously, for all these reasons and more, there is no space for non-Black children to ever use the N-word. It is our responsibility to teach our children *never* to use it. This also presents an opportunity to show our kids how to be allies and stand up against the use of the word when they hear it. Because they will. The true test will be how they respond when they do.

In order to teach them this, we have to explicitly state it. We need to share the history of the word—including the hurt that it causes, even to their friends who may not yet know why—in age-appropriate ways that reinforce the fact that this word is off-limits to us. If we don't clearly state that as a family, as a unit, we don't use the N-word because it is hateful, racist, and offensive, then our silence around the word may be misunderstood, as it has been for generations.

So be firm. Be clear. **Share the word's history with your kids, and share with others why that word is *never* okay to use in conversation, regardless of intent.** Because remember: It's the impact on the listener—not the intent—that matters. And in this case, the impact can *only* be violent and hateful.

CHAPTER 10

All Lives Matter, Blue Lives Matter

listen

Misasha has a Black Lives Matter magnet on her car. Her family made the decision to put the protest posters her kids made that say "Black Lives Matter, My Life Matters" at the bottom of their driveway, next to their mailbox, where others can see them as they go by in their cars, on their bikes, or on their daily walks. She sometimes sees people look twice at the car magnet, and she's definitely seen heads turn with regard to the driveway posters. She also admits to a strange unease when she parks near a police car—will they see her magnet? Will they really understand?

She's probably not alone.

When Black Lives Matter began and the voices of the movement came to occupy the center of our recent national discussion around race and systemic racism, it was inevitable that along with the supporters and agnostics or abstainers, there would be people who vehemently opposed their ideas and ideals. Maybe you saw opposition pop up on your social media feed. Maybe friends or colleagues or strangers used a common retort in response to articles you shared or told them about. Maybe it was a wisecrack or an angry remark about a T-shirt that you or someone else was wearing. But we're sure you heard it. We couldn't *stop* hearing it.

All lives matter.

Now think about how you felt, or feel, when you hear that phrase. Do you immediately feel indignant and think, that's not the point? Do you shrug your shoulders? Do you somewhat agree? Have you said that yourself?

You've also probably heard "Blue Lives Matter!" in response to a Black Lives Matter statement or protest as well. The Blue Lives Matter motto and countermovement emerged to advocate for police officers who had been killed in the line of duty or whose lives had been threatened. How do you feel when you hear that phrase?

Sit with this for a few minutes and really think about what emotions come to the forefront when you hear those phrases. Be honest with yourself. Because we're going to go into what #Black-LivesMatter means, where it came from, and how you can respond next time you hear these phrases.

learn

What do you really hear when you hear "Black Lives Matter"? Do you believe there's an implicit "only" in front of that statement? If so, you're not alone. But that's far from the truth.

Alicia Garza, one of the creators of the #BlackLivesMatter hashtag, explained in 2014 how Black lives mattering is a precondition for all lives mattering: **"Black Lives Matter doesn't mean your life isn't important—it means that Black lives, which are seen as without value within White supremacy, are important to your liberation.** Given the disproportionate impact state violence has on Black lives, we understand that when Black people in this country get free, the benefits will be wide-reaching and transformative for society as a whole. When we are able to end the hyper-criminalization and sexualization of Black people and end the poverty, control and surveillance of Black people, every single person in this world has a better shot at getting and staying free. **When Black people get free, everybody gets free."**

As one law professor put it when he was challenged by students who took offense to his Black Lives Matter T-shirt and wrote him an anonymous letter complaining that in fact "all lives matter": "There is a difference between focus and exclusion; if something matters, it does not mean that nothing else does." He did clarify that "there *are* some implicit words that precede 'Black Lives Matter,' and they go something like this: Because of the brutalizing and killing of Black people at the hands of the police and the indifference of society in general and the criminal justice system in particular, it is important that we say that. . . ."

In other words, the name of the movement was not chosen to mean that *only* Black lives matter. It's just that so many Black lives have been lived without due respect, safety, justice, fairness, attention, and equal opportunity for so long in this country that we need to focus on the need for change in the human condition in Black communities now in a way that we haven't for centuries.

So where did the Black Lives Matter movement come from, anyway?

The phrase "Black Lives Matter" was born in a July 13, 2013 Facebook post that community organizer Alicia Garza called a "love letter" to a broken Black community reeling after the acquittal of George Zimmerman for the murder of seventeen-year-old Trayvon Martin. In her post, Garza wrote: "the sad part is, there's a section of America who is cheering and celebrating right now, and that makes me sick to my stomach . . . btw stop saying we are not surprised. that's a damn shame in itself. I continue to be surprised at how little Black lives matter. And I will continue that. stop giving up on Black life . . . Black people. I love you. I love us. Our lives matter." Garza's friend Patrisse Cullors changed the last sentence to a hashtag—#BlackLivesMatter.

However, the birth of a hashtag didn't mean a movement was born immediately, or that the hashtag even went viral right away, as you probably know if you're a social media user. It took until the summer of 2014 and the death of another teenager—Michael Brown—at the hands of a White police officer in Ferguson, Missouri, for the hashtag and the movement to explode.

As noted by Pew Research: "The #BlackLivesMatter hashtag appeared an average of 58,747 times per day in the roughly three weeks following Brown's death. However, the use of the hashtag increased dramatically three months later when on November 25, the day after a Ferguson grand jury decided not to indict the officer involved in Brown's death, the #BlackLivesMatter hashtag appeared 172,772 times. During the subsequent three weeks, the hashtag was used 1.7 million times."

From that point forward, #BlackLivesMatter was a regular presence on Twitter, and would appear more frequently around additional murders or unjustified killings of Black people. In general, the use of the hashtag was in support of the sentiment underlying #BlackLivesMatter.

Oh yes, #AllLivesMatter and #BlueLivesMatter were also present on Twitter in this same space and time. Both hashtags have been used to push back against any focus on Black lives in social media from the inception of #BlackLivesMatter.

Fast-forward to July of 2016. One day apart, two men—Alton Sterling and Philando Castile—were murdered by police officers. In response, over the following several weeks, there were two attacks on law enforcement, one in Dallas, Texas, and one in Baton Rouge, Louisiana. Public sentiment started to shift, and people started using the #BlackLivesMatter hashtag to denounce the movement rather than support it as they previously had. In addition, the first signs of people linking #BlackLivesMatter with violence—and even terrorism—started to appear on Twitter. The effect was polarizing, with an onslaught of strident statements like "you're either with the police, or you're with Obama" and "you're with the police, or you're with #BlackLivesMatter."

As you can probably guess, this dichotomy was created in large part with the motive of forcing people to see themselves as either on the side of law and order (police) *or not* (#BlackLivesMatter). From there, it was easy to stretch and say that #BlackLivesMatter represented the opposite of law and order—that is, anarchy and terrorism.

Right? Wrong. Is Black Lives Matter a terrorist organization? NO. But the idea was contagious.

Even the FBI believed it. In fact, they were so concerned about the potential reach of the #BlackLivesMatter movement that in 2017 they invented a new domestic terrorism program category called the "Black Identity Extremist Movement," and used the existence of the program to justify surveilling people based solely on race.

As noted by the Brennan Center, "[i]n 2018 and 2019, the FBI conducted nationwide assessments of 'Black identity extremists' under an intelligence collection operation it called 'Iron Fist,' prioritizing these cases over investigations of far more prevalent violence from White supremacists and far right militants over that period, including mass shootings at a Pittsburgh synagogue and an El Paso shopping mall."

First of all, "Iron Fist" sounds like the scariest operation ever. Second, and more importantly, while the FBI was focusing attention, money, and equipment on these "assessments," it missed investigating clear instances of mass violence—mass violence that was perpetrated by White people and were clear acts of domestic terrorism.

As it turned out, the FBI spent a lot of time and money investigating #BlackLivesMatter but found no terrorist threat there. In contrast, in the month after George Floyd was murdered, North Carolina lawyer T. Greg Doucette and mathematician Jason Miller compiled a data set of more than five hundred incidents of police violence against protesters, captured on video by activists and journalists, since Floyd's death. Again, that's the one-month count. Not surprisingly, that occurrence rate was significantly higher than any accounts of violence directed against police by Black Lives Matter protesters, or even Antifa.

As we write, just weeks before the 2020 general election in America, Black Lives Matter leaders are having to address death threats that they are receiving from White supremacist groups. They're not the ones issuing them—that is what terrorists do. They're the ones who are fighting to keep their families and their own Black bodies safe, yet again.

act

So, you've got a friend who sees your "Black Lives Matter" T-shirt and immediately responds with, "But all lives matter." What do you say?

Sometimes highlighting what each statement really means helps. You may have already heard some analogies that explain why that response is missing the point. We've got a couple of favorites we'd like to share here.

The first analogy is perhaps Misasha's favorite, partly due to the fact that she lives in a high fire-threat district: A house is on fire. While firefighters are trying to battle the blaze that may burn this house to the ground, does it make sense to stand there and yell, "All houses matter!" to get those firefighters to focus on all of the other houses? If the other houses aren't in immediate danger, and definitely aren't on fire, then resources should be directed at the house that is *actually* on fire . . . right? Because hosing down or trying to save a house that isn't on fire doesn't make any sense. That house isn't in danger. That house is fine. We have to direct our attention to help the house that may not survive the blaze. #BlackLivesMatter.

The second analogy is equally relatable. You're attending a breast cancer fundraiser. Maybe it's a Susan G. Komen black-tie affair and you've donated money to help support funding and research for a cancer that is still killing many people. Your donation is specific to breast cancer, not to any other kind of cancer. Yes, breast cancer mainly affects women, and yes, it only affects a subset of women. Does it make sense to walk into that fundraiser and yell "All cancers matter!"? We don't think so. Sometimes there are issues that are specific to a certain group of people, and *those people and those people alone* need our immediate help. #BlackLivesMatter.

How about when you hear someone say "Blue Lives Matter," or you hear about a Blue Lives Matter protest? First, it's important to note that police aren't blue, in that their skin color isn't blue. So at the end of the day, when they take off their uniforms, they are who they are under that uniform. **Black people don't have the ability to, or the luxury of, taking off their Black skin in any scenario.** They're Black 24/7. Based on that fact alone, the comparison between Black and blue lives simply doesn't equate.

But again—it's important to emphasize that by saying #BlackLivesMatter, we are not saying *only* #BlackLivesMatter. We do believe the men and women who serve as police officers also have lives that are important. But we know that police kill Black people at a much higher rate than they're killing everyone else. We need to focus our attention on the group that is struggling to survive.

Perhaps this is a way to think about this issue: **In our search for "equality," we must remember that in a fundamental way, we**

do not start out equal. Not in this country; not yet, anyway. It's up to us now to make sure that we help those who need our help the most, if we're truly trying to get to equality. And just as important, if not more so, is sharing and reinforcing this understanding and these goals with our children. #BlackLivesMatter.

CHAPTER 11

Driving While Black

listen ⎯⎯⎯⎯⎯⎯⎯⎯⎯⎯⎯⎯⎯⎯⎯⎯⎯⎯⎯⎯⎯⎯⎯⎯

You might be familiar with this story, but we think it's worth telling again. Philando Castile was in the car with his girlfriend, Diamond Reynolds, and Reynolds's four-year-old daughter on the evening of July 6, 2016, in Falcon Heights, Minnesota. He was stopped by a police officer, Jeronimo Yanez, because his taillight was out.

In the span of 40 seconds, what should have been a routine traffic stop escalated into murder. As documented by the dashboard camera on the police cruiser, Yanez approached the car and asked for Castile's driver's license and insurance. The ensuing seconds were all captured on video, and shown later as part of Yanez's day in court, but the part of the conversation that takes place between them for 10 short seconds is the one that ends up killing Philando Castile.

Thirty seconds into the conversation, Castile begins to tell Yanez that he has a weapon.

Castile: Sir, I have to tell you I do have a . . .

Yanez: OK.

Castile: . . . firearm on me.

Yanez: OK

Castile: I (inaudible)

Yanez: Don't reach for it, then.

Castile: I'm, I, I was reaching for . . .

Yanez: Don't pull it out.

Castile: I'm not pulling it out.

Reynolds: He's not.

Yanez: Don't pull it out.

At that point, Yanez, who had his hand near his gun, pulls out his weapon and fires seven times into the car, hitting Castile five times. At that point, Reynolds yells, "You just killed my boyfriend!" and Castile gasps, "I wasn't reaching. . . ."

It's too late. Philando Castile was killed in the street at thirty-two years old.

Unfortunately, Philando Castile's story isn't unique. Not any part of it. Not if you're Black.

Not the part about being stopped for a routine traffic stop, not the part about the officer having his hand close to his gun, not the part about the officer shooting him.

None of it.

You never get the benefit of the doubt in a situation like this—if you're Black. And it's more likely to happen to you if you're Black than any other race in America.

learn ──────────────────────

Driving While Black: DWB. Let's break it down.

There have been a number of recent studies and books that have captured data showing that yes, in fact, Black and Brown drivers are stopped—and searched—at a rate disproportionate to the numbers of total drivers, even considering other factors (time of day, location, etc.). The Stanford Open Policing Project, which is a partnership between the Stanford Computational Journalism Lab, the Knight Foundation, and the Stanford Computational Policy Lab, has been requesting data regarding traffic stops and searches from across the country since 2015. As of this writing, the project has collected and standardized *over 200 million* such records, which point to the disproportionate rate of Black and Hispanic drivers being stopped, but also to the power of policy interventions which could help reduce the racial disparities inherent in our current system.

A similar study was conducted by ABC News in collaboration with ABC-owned stations, which analyzed data collected by local police departments on millions of traffic stops over the past several years. According to the 2020 report issued by ABC news, Black drivers (or even Black pedestrians) were more likely to be stopped by police than White drivers or pedestrians in a number of American cities, even after accounting for the demographics of the cities and counties these police departments serve.

Now, your first reaction when reading this might be—well, just because there are disparities in how drivers are stopped, that doesn't necessarily mean that there's racial bias. And that is true in that one can't prove the other.

However, what the data does show (and we love some good data over here!) is that there are often huge discrepancies in how one city's police force addresses Black people compared with White people, all other things roughly equal. According to ABC News, in Minneapolis, Black drivers were five times more likely to be stopped by police than White drivers. In Chicago and San Francisco, Black drivers were four times more likely to be stopped. And in Philadelphia and Los Angeles, Black drivers were about three times more likely to be stopped.

The difference in how often Black versus White drivers are stopped by police also extends to what happens after they are stopped. ABC News noted that in all nine cities where search-conduct data was available, their analysis found that Black drivers were more likely to be searched during stops than White drivers. And in four cities (Philadelphia, Chicago, Fresno, and San Francisco), Black drivers who were stopped were less likely to be found possessing contraband than White drivers.

If you're thinking that there must have been cities where it was found that Black and White drivers were equally likely to be stopped—you're right. Louisville, Kentucky, and Houston, Texas, according to ABC News. But, as we now know, being stopped is not the end of the story. Even in those two cities, according to

ABC News, Black drivers were treated differently than their White counterparts. For example, in Houston, Black drivers were three times more likely than White drivers to be searched after being stopped by police. And in Louisville, Black drivers "were more likely to be stopped for suspected violations that turned out to not be serious enough to lead officers to issue the driver a citation."

MICROAGGRESSION: Locking your car door when a Black person comes close

You might think the rate at which Black drivers are being pulled over and searched is unfair, even unethical. But it doesn't end there. The result of this disparity in traffic stops and searches creates a ripple effect throughout the entire criminal justice system. Let's play this out.

Traffic stops often result in traffic tickets, which result in fines or fees due. As ABC News reports, the failure to pay those fines and fees can result in the suspension of drivers' licenses and in many cases an "impossible choice," according to Joanna Weiss, the cofounder and the codirector of Fines and Fees Justice Center, a nonprofit advocacy organization who looks into the impact of these stops on the larger justice system.

So let's say you got pulled over for DWB. You were issued a ticket, which you can't afford to pay right now, and your license is suspended. What do you do?

Choice number 1: You have to stop driving, which means no way to get to work, childcare, healthcare, and possibly basic necessities like grocery stores and pharmacies. That option doesn't seem sustainable—but what choice do you have?

Choice number 2: You keep driving, and risk being pulled over again. You do get pulled over, and this time it results in a misdemeanor charge because you're driving on a suspended license. That also means higher fines and fees, and maybe even jail time.

Suddenly, one traffic stop has spiraled into a permanent record and you are being inextricably linked (in a negative, irreversible way) with the criminal justice system. And all because—and *just* because—you're Black.

And remember—that's if you're lucky. Because you're still able to walk away.

DWB and Criminal Justice

Let's now talk about *why* police officers often stop Black motorists. It's not just because they may have violated some minor traffic law. It's because the police officer has the ability to stop drivers for a minor offense when they actually believe there's a bigger offense that's been committed, like drug possession. This is called a pretext stop, and it's been sanctioned by the Supreme Court.

The obvious problem with pretext stops is that, unlike what the name suggests, police don't really need an actual pretext to stop drivers. There are so many vague traffic laws out there that it's not hard to find one that allows police to pull over drivers—particularly Black ones—if they can claim they were actually looking for more.

And that "more"? It's typically related to illegal possession of contraband. Or suspicion of contraband possession. Statistics from a traffic survey conducted in North Carolina highlight just how much more of an issue this is in Black traffic stops than White ones.

In the book *Suspect Citizens: What 20 Million Traffic Stops Tell Us About Policing and Race*, the authors found that, on a national average, Black drivers were 63 percent more likely to be stopped even though, as a whole, they drive 16 percent less. If you factor time on the road in, Black drivers were 95 percent more likely to be stopped. In addition, Black drivers were 115 percent more likely than White drivers to be searched in a traffic stop; yet, contraband was more likely to be found in searches of *White* drivers.

What does this all mean? Well, simply put, Black drivers are more likely to be stopped. They're more likely to be searched. But they're *not* the ones more likely to have contraband, statistically, so that means that pretext stops, if you're drawing the whole idea to its natural conclusion, aren't based solely on an actual suspicion of contraband possession. They're based on race, with contraband possession being a nice-to-have along the way.

You can imagine, though—similar to the traffic fees and fines and penalties that attach when Black drivers are more frequently stopped than White drivers—that when Black drivers actually do have contraband in their possession, the criminal justice system in this country is also fully stacked against them, largely because of the link between poverty, race, and mass incarceration.

Each part of the justice system is set up to fail Black people. Bail alone is an almost insurmountable hurdle if you're poor. The median felony bail bond amount ($10,000) is the equivalent of eight months' income for the typical detained defendant. And Black Americans, who face much greater rates of poverty, also make up much more of the nation's prison population than they should—40 percent of the incarcerated population are Black, whereas only 13 percent of all of the residents of the United States are Black.

act

So what can you do about all of this, besides be upset by the inequities that Black people face every time they decide to get behind the wheel? Well, if you work in law enforcement, you can absolutely look into your department's policies and procedures around pretext stops. In fact, anyone can look into their state's stance on pretext stops, and vote for measures that would ban racially charged ways to differentiate people based solely on a "suspicion of guilt."

But what can you do on a personal level, when you see something like this happen? Because we've all been there—you see the flashing lights of the police car behind you, you hold your breath, and then you let it out in one big whoosh when you realize the police car is pulling over the car next to you, or the car in front of you. But what if you then drive by and realize that the exchange isn't going well, or you see someone whose voice may not be being heard?

First, you'll want to be safe. But second, if you can, be an upstander. Use the White privilege that you have to ask questions. To stand up for fairness and justice. To record with your cell phone if something feels off to you. To call for help. To ask if you can be of help. Be a witness. Be a voice. Don't just drive by, if you're able to stop. Remember that only a fraction of the racially charged incidents that we hear about are recorded—so help spread the word and awareness. And equip your kids with the same tools that you now possess so that they feel empowered to be an upstander like you (in an age and situation appropriate manner). After they've witnessed you acting on the right side of justice, follow up with a conversation at home about how they might safely do the same at school, around the neighborhood, or at soccer practice.

Because remember that breath you let out when you realized you were safe? That's something that most Black people can't do in this scenario—including, perhaps, Misasha's husband and boys—because if they get behind the wheel, they'll always be DWB. We can help change that, if we remain vigilant and stand up for others.

CHAPTER 12

But that Looting, Though . . .

listen

On March 3, 1991, a motorist named Rodney King was pulled over by California Highway Patrol officers as he was speeding on a freeway in Los Angeles. According to the Associated Press, King tried to get away from the police, partly because he had been drinking and partly because he was out of jail on probation for a robbery conviction, but he finally pulled over and stopped his car in front of a San Fernando Valley apartment building. George Holliday, who lived in the apartment building and heard the noise when the traffic stop happened, came outside and videotaped the interaction (remember how we just said be an upstander? This is a perfect example of doing just that).

What his videotape showed was shocking to so many Americans, of all races including the large White majority: Four White officers beat and kicked King dozens of times, even after he was down on the ground. Holliday gave the tape to a local TV station and the tape went viral—and this was before social media was a thing. Total mass outrage ensued. The officers were charged, and the case went to trial.

But, as we're unfortunately used to seeing, justice wasn't exactly served. On April 29, 1992, after seven days of deliberations, the jury acquitted all four officers of assault, and acquitted three of the four officers from using excessive force (they couldn't agree on a verdict for the fourth officer charged). Total mass outrage ensued again, this time in the form of the Los Angeles Riots.

On April 29, 1992, Misasha was a freshman in high school in Pasadena, a suburb of Los Angeles, and was busy setting up after school for their annual Pet and Hobby Show. She vaguely remembers hearing from the school office that her dad was coming to pick her up, which was a news event in and of itself, as her dad mostly came to school on Back-to-School nights. By the time he pulled up, the sky was getting dark. Not because night was falling. From fires. It was still mid-afternoon.

What she remembers happening over those next few days shaped her memories and concepts of what riots and looting meant: Fear that looters and rioters were coming to her neighborhood (they did, but stores were boarded up already and looting was limited). Watching the Korean store owners stand on their store roofs with loaded guns, prepared to defend their property against looters. Seeing Black people on TV rioting, looting, and stealing. For these several days, the lines drawn between the suburbs, 'hoods, and cities were blurred in Los Angeles. The violence was widespread enough so that it theoretically *could* happen to anyone, but in reality, it mainly happened to and in the communities that were already the most impacted by the bias and inequities responsible for what had originally happened to Rodney King.

The images told a story that the news and the media were eager to repackage and sell to all of us. It was one of destruction borne of pain and frustration, but destruction nonetheless. It was minorities pitted against minorities, and neighbors destroying neighborhoods. It was poor people grabbing what they could take with a complete disregard for the law. It was a narrative that Misasha took with her into adulthood.

But it wasn't the right narrative.

learn

In looking back at the Rodney King riots, and then at the very recent media analysis in the aftermath of George Floyd's murder, we can see that the stories that we have told ourselves often leave out the *why*. **Why would Black people loot and riot, in response to a perceived injustice, if it only hurts them?**

As we all know, the Rodney King beating wasn't the first tragic event to engage America in this conversation with regard to demonstrations of civil unrest. That conversation has been going on for hundreds of years and is directly tied to systemic racism in this country. When one group of people oppresses another group, the outlets afforded that oppressed group to express their voices and be heard shrink considerably.

In a dramatic pinnacle of the twentieth century, America saw issues of racial equality take center stage throughout the 1960s and the Civil Rights movement in this country. Major cities burned from 1964 through 1966, and the "Long Hot Summer" of July 1967 saw 163 cities "erupt in collective violence" with regard to the very same issues as in 2020: police brutality and general indifference to Black suffering.

The effects of the 1960s riots? Death was one—and not from the rioters. In Newark, New Jersey, thirty-four people died, twenty-three at the hands of the largely White police force. In Detroit, that death toll was higher, as forty-three people died, most of them shot by seventeen thousand police (again, largely White), National Guard, and military troops sent to put down the rebellion.

The riots didn't end, though. And neither did police brutality and general indifference to Black suffering. In 1968, a White racist man shot and killed Martin Luther King Jr. According to National Geographic, that sorrow and fury "turned into [a national] uprising in which more than 100 cities were burned." Looting was also a result of this national pain. In studying these events of 1968, sociologists Russell Dynes and E. L. Quarantelli wrote, in their groundbreaking study, that "the looting that takes place in these situations is usually interpreted as evidence of human depravity."

That is definitely how we heard it being discussed in 2020. We heard it from our own circles. If everyone just stayed peaceful and calm, and protested in a manner that people felt comfortable with seeing, then White Americans would support these types of protests and calls for justice.

So let us ask a question.

When the pain and suffering of your people has been largely devalued for centuries, when you bring attention to problems by taking a knee during the national anthem and then see a man suffocated to death by a knee on his neck, when you protest peacefully and your children and leaders are shot by the police on the streets, when this happens over and over again—what would you do next? Would you say, "Well, let's just keep this peaceful and things will change one day. Even though we've been trying this tactic over the last four hundred years and we've gotten . . . not very far"?

Yeah, we didn't think so. (Us neither, for the record)

But in order to understand more about the motivations behind violence in situations like this, we also need to understand a few concepts.

First, as Dana Fisher, a sociologist at the University of Maryland notes, peaceful protestors and looters are often two distinct groups, and typically individuals are not drawn into the group that is not theirs when witnessing each other's tactics, even if in the same physical space. As she puts it in the *Atlantic*, "I've never seen somebody come in who's peaceful and then it's like, *Hey, they just broke that window over there. I'm going to now start looting. . . .*"

But it's also important to understand that even the group of looters seemingly united in their motives in social unrest often have different agendas. When you think about the Black looters and violent protesters in the Civil Rights era, and again during the summer of George Floyd's murder, why do you think they loot? To steal things? Perhaps—in extremely poor areas, it may feel like a way to "level the playing field" after years and years of frustration around inequities based on systemic racism has built up and then boils over in the areas that signify everything that the looters don't have. It's almost like a seizing of reparations for the decades of wrongdoing and punishment they've suffered due to factors largely out of their control, in a society that's stacked against them from the start.

Robert C. Smith, an emeritus professor of political science at San Francisco State University, agrees, as he said in *USA Today*: "What if looting is an organic expression of rage—lashing out not just against police abuses, but against the historic legacy of a societal knee on the neck? [. . .] What if . . . big-box stores and swanky malls were targeted not just because they have really nice stuff, but because they are perceived as symbols of economic inequality and institutional racism?" **Once you start thinking about history and looting together, the violence behind looting takes on a different tone entirely.**

Dynes and Quarantelli also found that vandalism during protests is often centered around significant locations and things—"objects and buildings that are 'symbolic of other values,'" like the authority that a police car represents. As Olga Khazan notes in her article in the *Atlantic*, "[i]n this way, some of the looting is a lashing-out against capitalism, the police, and other forces that are seen as perpetuating racism." In other words, the system is broken, and it will continue to destroy marginalized communities unless they fight back.

One last note on the *why* behind looting: Sometimes looting is done *just because*, and often not by the affected groups. You may remember the "umbrella man" in Minneapolis in the wake of George Floyd, who was accused of inciting riots and looting in the city. It was only after the fact that the entire country learned it was actually a thirty-two-year-old White supremacist behind the mask and umbrella, not a Black man as (mostly White) people had assumed. So sometimes, sadly, looting is just that. Violence for violence sake.

But we challenge you to think bigger when you hear about looting. Is it violence? Or is it an outlet for an otherwise unheard, marginalized community when the pressure is just too much to bear? As noted by the *Atlantic*, and as one looter, Pamela Speaks, told the *Miami Herald* during the 1992 Los Angeles riots, "I don't think it's right, but it gets the frustrations out."

act

Think about the why. Use your desire to understand and those critical thinking skills that we know you have—because those are what drove you to pick up this book—and challenge your first gut reaction when you hear about violence, looting, and rioting in the aftermath of a particularly terrible incident. **We have entire communities in our country that live in pain, and when the daily persistence of that pain gets to be too much, what should we expect?**

Be careful when you read or listen to mainstream media or social media pages that depict looting in a one-dimensional way. Because now you know that it's not a singular story. You should, however, listen to the painful truths directly from the mouths of others who have their lived experiences to share. Of course we cannot solve everything, but we can hear and validate the pain of others. So please, try to do just that.

Once you've thought about the why—**talk about the why.** Share your thoughts and insights with your personal spheres of power, be they professional, personal, your kids, your church group, your book club, whatever—deepen the discussion by discussing not just the acts, but the possible motivations behind them. Using phrases like "I wonder . . ." "or "I believe . . . but what do you think?" can be extremely helpful because that way you not only open up a dialogue, you keep the focus on what *you* think, which may allow your listener to put down some of their natural defenses (which we all have) from the start.

See how you (and perhaps your family) can help. One of the ways that our national conversation around the police has changed recently is we are reimagining the role of the police. What if we had a more "community policing" approach to daytime protests, which often are more amicable, less violent? Violence begets violence—so when police react with bullets and riot gear, their presence shifts the tone of a peaceful gathering radically, or adds a show of violence to a protest that's already building tensions. And when that happens, what is our ultimate goal? Is it more violence? Or is it to have people's concerns be heard and addressed? (We'd reckon the latter, but . . .) If measures like community policing, which would include key tenets like community organizations working in tandem with the police, organizational transformation on the part of policing agencies, and proactive problem solving to address community needs before police need to get involved, appear on the ballots on voting day, vote for them. Or petition to get them into your communities.

And finally—hold the media accountable for the narrative that they spread as well. Be vocal. Write letters. Demand better. **Share the why, and we may be in a very different place when next faced with national social unrest.**

CHAPTER 13

Gang Violence and Black-on-Black Crime

listen ——————————————————

Caylin Moore is a college graduate. He was a 2017 Rhodes Scholar. He did his graduate studies at Oxford (yes, the one in England). He's an author. In the fall of 2020, he started his PhD studies at Stanford University.

He's also twenty-four, Black, and from Compton, California, a city with a complex history of high crime and homicide rates.

He might not be who you're picturing when we talk about gangs and Black-on-Black violence, but that's the world he came from.

We had Caylin as a guest on the podcast back in the late summer of 2020, and during that recording he talked about his memory of being on the playground in kindergarten the year that his family moved to Compton. Two other kids were discussing what they were going to do *when*—not if—they went to prison. Can you imagine that conversation between White kids? Or in your neighborhood?

In middle school, he got in trouble because he wasn't bringing books to school. Why? It wasn't that Caylin wasn't a dedicated student; he had to ride the bus, and the route to his school went right through several gang territories. He wanted to be light on his feet in case he had to run or got jumped. A heavy backpack filled with books would weigh him down. This was the world that Caylin came from. He made it out—but many others do not. And many of them become the gang members that you may know only from movies, or rap albums.

What do you think of when you hear the word "gang"? Do you picture a group of men? Boys? And what race are they? If you hear the word "gang" and you immediately picture a Black man wearing Crips colors or Bloods colors, you're probably not alone. That's definitely the image we've been indoctrinated in through the media. A myriad of popular movies depict brutal gang violence, Black man against Black man, and so we may nod our heads along with the next person who says to us, "Well, what about Black-on-Black crime?" because those are images we understand.

It's a convenient narrative, and one that largely doesn't have to affect us, perhaps, if we're not Black. But is it the *full* narrative? Let's go in a little deeper.

learn

So, next question. Did you see *Gangs of New York*? In this 2002 Martin Scorcese film loosely based on the nonfiction book by the same name by Herbert Asbury, Leonardo di Caprio plays a member of a gang who is looking to avenge his father's gang-related death years earlier. That's not just the film's story, though—it's part of the real history of New York, where in the nineteenth century, prior to Prohibition and the domination of the Mafia, gangs of largely White immigrants ruled the streets of the city. There were numerous actual gangs with names like the Dead Rabbits (di Caprio's in the film) and the Nativist Protestants who were deeply divided by culture and religion. But all of them were what we would consider White today. And New York isn't the only city with this story.

Historians James C. Howell and John P. Moore discuss how the first "street gangs" in our country appeared in the Northeast and the Midwest. While the reasons behind their arrival simmered within a different time and circumstance, the formative forces were the same as those that led to Black gangs in the United States years later:

White Street Gangs

"Gang emergence . . . was fueled by immigration and poverty, first by two waves of poor, largely White families from Europe. Seeking a better life, the early immigrant groups mainly settled in urban areas and formed communities to join each other in the economic struggle. Unfortunately, they had few marketable skills. Difficulties in finding work and a place to live and adjusting to urban life were equally common among the European immigrants. Anglo native-born Americans discriminated against these immigrants as well. Conflict was therefore imminent, and gangs grew in such environments."

In other words, these gangs made up of poor, immigrant White people were essentially formed as survival mechanisms. They were composed of people who needed to figure out a way to navigate their new home where they found society largely shut them out, and had to create their own means of economic success in order to do so. The massive influx of these groups of immigrants into cities meant that housing was scarce, jobs even scarcer, and when coupled with the discrimination—and often threats of bodily harm— they faced, they almost had no other choice but to band together in order not to die.

In New York, the gangs were started as a social network. "Many street gang members were employed, mostly as common laborers. Some were bouncers in saloons and dance halls, as well as long-shoremen. A few were apprentice butchers, carpenters, sailmakers, and shipbuilders. They engaged in violence, but violence was a normal part of their always-contested environment; turf warfare was a condition of the neighborhood." Gangs formed the "basic unit of social life among the young males in New York in the nineteenth century." However, there were gangs that soon turned criminal, seeing opportunity in illegal contraband that was kind of like a get-rich-quick scheme at the time. Indeed, the Five Points gang that's referenced in the film *Gangs of New York* (and is central to the book) has been called the most significant street gang ever to be formed in America, as it became not only a training ground for the Mafia, but also provided bodyguard and enforcement muscle to politicians at the time.

After the first wave of gangs in New York City, Howell and Moore note, "[t]he arrival of the Poles, Italians, and Jews in New York City in the period 1880–1920 ushered in a second distinct period of gang activity in the city's slums." In Chicago, White immigrants began forming their own gangs along ethnic lines prior to the Civil War. In the West, Mexican immigrants and migration patterns— beginning in Mexico, winding through Texas and New Mexico, and ending up in Los Angeles—created "boy gangs" around the 1890s, comprised of groups of men, largely outcasts in their own natu- ralized country (as many had become American citizens), but still feeling as though the United States had stolen much of that part of the country from Mexico. This "physical and cultural marginaliza- tion" was the driving reason behind gang formation at this point, according to Howell and Moore.

Non-White Street Gangs

So, the history of gangs in our country is a complicated one from the start, but one that's filled with White people and, as our coun- try expanded farther West, groups of people with origins from Mexico and other Latin American countries. How did we get to a gang narrative that largely focuses just on Black and Brown people, then?

Systemic racism.

Maybe it's easiest to explain if we look at one city over a period of decades. Let's take as our example South Central Los Angeles, which is close to (yet so far from) Misasha's hometown of Pasadena and also the longtime home of those gangs we talked about at the beginning of this chapter—the Crips and the Bloods. It's also Caylin Moore's home, the young scholar from Compton, California, who we introduced earlier.

In a useful and powerful capsule history called "Timeline: South Central Los Angeles" from the PBS blog *Independent Lens*, we see that in 1941, President Roosevelt loosened some racial restrictions on jobs in order to get more workers in wartime industries, which meant that Black Americans suddenly had a lot more job options. Companies including Goodyear, Firestone, and Ford set up facto- ries in South Los Angeles. Between 1940 and 1970, five million Black people left the South for the North and the West. In this time period, Los Angeles's Black population increased more than tenfold—from 63,744 people to nearly 736,000.

Sounds great, right? Jobs, opportunities, and more people. Los Angeles was thriving.

But there were restrictions, even in the immediate postwar era. The newly named "South Central" was the only district in Los Angeles where Black people were legally allowed to own property. Due to racially restrictive housing covenants (which were enforced not only legally, or by the police, but also by White homeowners), Los Angeles's schools and communities were segregated, with many people of color denied the right to own homes.

In 1948, the Supreme Court struck down these racial housing bans in *Shelley v. Kraemer*, which allowed Black people to buy homes outside of South Central. However, this coincided nicely with the growth and expansion of the Los Angeles freeway system. White people started moving to the suburbs, especially when a technique called "blockbusting" was employed, a practice whereby Black people were "introduced" to White neighborhoods to "spark rapid White flight and housing price decline." Using this strategy, property developers introduced one Black family into a previously all-White neighborhood, then started rumors among the White families there about impending home and property depreciation as a result. Soon enough, those rumors would turn into reality as White people would sell their homes, often for under market value, in order to get out of a potentially even worse situation—at least one that they believed would be worse, based on those rumors . . . yes, systemic racism. Blockbusting worked like a charm, and kept Los Angeles highly segregated, with Black people now living in increasingly poorer, urban areas while White people moved out en masse to the suburbs.

> **MICROAGGRESSION: Checking your purse or wallet when a person with darker skin approaches**

And, as you might imagine, this racial divide and very obvious segregation illuminated already heightened racial tensions. In response to White violence against Black people who went into White neighborhoods, young Black men formed street clubs such as the Devil Hunters, the Farmers, and the Huns. Violence was interracial—White gangs versus Black gangs, with many of the Black gangs organized according to the housing projects they lived in within South Los Angeles.

As populations grew, public housing proliferated. As of the late 1950s, the largest housing projects west of the Mississippi were located in South Central; the neighborhood of Watts was one-third public housing. Although the Civil Rights Act allowed for federal regulations around racial segregation, states (including California) enacted their own laws to get around housing restrictions. This, in turn, created further racial disparity in housing, leaving Black residents with increasingly poorer and more precarious options.

The Watts riots in 1965, which pitted police against Black residents, was another turning point in the city's history, as after the riots, Black street clubs in South Los Angeles began to organize against police brutality. Following the riots, the "Black Power Movement gained strength nationally, and violent gang activity decreased in Los Angeles, as former members of gangs . . . joined up with the Black Panther Party (BPP), the US Organization, and other socially conscious groups." Seeing this, the FBI, working in conjunction with the LAPD, "intimidated, incarcerated, and assassinated many of the movement's leaders." The FBI also orchestrated violence between the different groups, causing the murder of at least two BPP leaders in 1969.

Crips and Bloods

The lasting effects of White flight directly contributed to the decline in South Central's quality of living and the rise of the Bloods and the Crips in the 1970s. "With many Black political leaders imprisoned or marginalized, African American youth in South Central were left without role models in the community, and the number of street gangs increased. A gang called the Baby Avenues was started by 15-year-old Raymond Washington, in emulation of the Black Panthers and to fill the void left by the waning Black Power movement. Due to its members' youthfulness, the gang became known as the Avenue Cribs, which later morphed into 'Crips.'"

As the Crips gained power, other gangs formed an alliance to stop them, and the Bloods were born. By 1972, there were ten more gangs in South Central, and in that year twenty-nine gang-related murders in Los Angeles, then an all-time high. But by 1974, gang-related murders numbered seventy, and the Crips and the Bloods control South Central LA, Compton, and Inglewood, an area of roughly thirty square miles.

Not surprisingly, the rise in gang numbers was directly tied to employment opportunities drying up due to the continued White flight and perceived and actual dangers present in the area. Between 1978 and 1982, 101 new Black gangs formed in Los Angeles. During that same time period, seventy thousand workers would be laid off in South Los Angeles.

In 1981, crack cocaine came to South Central, thereby pushing an already extremely segregated, oppressed community over the edge. The Bloods and the Crips were increasingly involved in the drug's production, as well as sales, which led to increasing violence and neighborhood destruction. These factors, along with the Reagan era policies folded into a campaign called the War on Drugs, led to a skyrocketing rate of incarceration of Black men and boys.

You might know where this is going. By 2003, one in four Black men were sent to prison in their lifetime. California had at that time the largest number of female prisoners in the United States, most of whom were mothers of young children. Arguably, this particular statistic was largely due to smaller, civilian "wars on drugs" that were waged in communities like South Central where desperate mothers looked for ways to feed their children— and, without alternatives, the drug trade was sometimes the only option.

And those who were left? As the *Independent Lens* "Timeline" notes, by the mid-2000s, "[g]enerations of project residents had gone without jobs and economic opportunities and 75 percent of the neighborhood's adult African American males would be incarcerated in their lifetimes. Watts residents had a 1 in 250 chance of being murdered—in comparison to 1 in 18,000 for average Americans—and nearly half of the neighborhood's children suffered from post-traumatic stress disorder."

Just sit with those statistics for a second. When you are born into a neighborhood like this, a neighborhood that has been shaped by gang violence borne directly from racism and segregation, what are your options? Sure, some well-meaning programs were put in place—for a year or so—to try and help South Los Angeles. But not enough, and not those that really addressed the roots of the problem: again, systemic racism.

As you and I both know now, gangs were and are more than just a survival mechanism—they allow members to thrive both socially, through finding a "family" which helps to ensure their safety, and economically—unfortunately often through the sale of drugs or other substances. Thus, that thriving is often limited by extreme penalties around drug possession and sale, and a criminal justice system designed to put and keep Black people, especially Black men, in jails and prisons for extended periods of time.

And the reasons why those gangs were created in the first place? Systemic racism, which promoted and supported poverty, segregation, unequal opportunity and quality of life, restrictions on freedoms and basic services, and police brutality, all driven by White fear and prejudice and often aggression. Black gangs, in turn, formed to protect Black communities from racism in all of its ugly forms.

Black-on-Black Crime

Now we come to the second subject of this chapter: Black-on-Black crime. You may have heard this term, as it's been co-opted by the anti–Black Lives Matter movement, or the anti–Defund the Police movement, to highlight a statistic that Black people kill more Black people than White people kill Black people. Unfortunately, that's true. But it's equally true (and unfortunate) that White people kill more White people than Black people do.

The Bureau of Justice Statistics' 2016 crime victimization statistics report (updated in 2018) shows those who commit violent acts tend to commit them against members of the same race as the offender. Offenders were White in 62 percent of violent incidents committed against White victims, Black in 70 percent of incidents committed against Black victims, and Hispanic in 45 percent of incidents committed against Hispanic victims, according to the BJS report.

Yet Black-on-Black crime is consistently alone in the spotlight, often serving as a justification for aggressive policing of the Black community as well as the much higher incarceration rate for Black individuals.

That's not to say that there isn't a high rate of Black-on-Black crime. There is. We just talked about the rise of gangs as a survival mechanism, and that is one definite source of Black-on-Black crime. But the problem comes when it's being used to suppress awareness and deny the existence of systemic racism, like Donald Trump tried to do during his 2016 campaign for President, just like many other politicians before him.

Because remember those White gangs at the start of this chapter? They got help. When you think about that postwar economic boom that caused a lot of Black people to move West—they weren't the beneficiaries of a lot of the government programs that were designed to create that American middle class. Black people were purposefully cut out of the GI Bill—the bill that was designed to make sure all returning veterans after World War II were given benefits that included education and practical training. Black people didn't get the VA benefits that should have come along with the GI Bill, nor did they benefit from FHA housing (see page 32). These stimulus efforts to create a stable middle class were not necessarily altruistic; they were designed as a bailout for White people, to create economic security for White people to the exclusion of Black people. It worked out well for White people.

Not so much for Black people, as we detailed above in our South Central example (see page 134). And that's just one city, in one state; this was happening all over the country. So when you're thinking about Black-on-Black violence, and the *why* behind it—you simply cannot leave systemic racism out of the equation.

act ———————————————————— 🔊

You might have read all of this and thought, I've seen *Boyz n the Hood*. I donate to community organizations. What else can I do? Here are some ideas.

First, do your research. A lot of the systemic issues of oppression and hopelessness come from the high incarceration rate of Black people, especially Black men, in areas that are already hit hard by gangs. Look at who your prosecutors and judges are. How do they deal with crime? How do they deal with systemic issues? How do they work with the police? **Know and vote for the prosecutors and judges who are there to help destroy, not cement, the system that perpetuates Black violence and Black persecution.**

Follow federal policy that will help as well—familiarizing yourself with the First Step Act is a great place to start, as there are accountability measures contained in there, and metrics that the DOJ is supposed to be reporting back on. Your attorney general is tasked with enforcing the First Step Act, so it's important to know who yours is, and where they stand on issues like these.

These are the people who may be still in office when your kids are adults, but even if they're not, they're going to shape the laws and policies that will directly affect your kids' generation.

Second, remember the difference between being an ally and being an accomplice. Here's where you want to start being an accomplice, if you haven't been yet. You want to help dismantle systems of oppression, but take your cues directly from the group being oppressed—here, it's Black people in impoverished communities. **Do your research into which programs are being run by the community, not just *for* the community.** Those are the programs where you should donate time and, if possible, money. Hint: Do your research thoroughly when choosing where to offer your help; mutual aid networks and participatory grant-making organizations are often more community-driven and less tied to the White savior industrial complex (see page 34) than many nonprofits.

Third, speak up. When someone tosses out, "Well, Black people kill more Black people than police do" or, "Gang violence is what's destroying the Black community," now you know why that's the case—and it's not because Black people hate other Black people. It often comes down to the lack of hope due to the systemic lack of choices available to Black people. Talk about the why behind the lack of hope—the systemic racism, White flight and block-busting and perpetuation of Black people as second-class citizens.

Ask questions to make people think critically about why there are instances when Black people do kill other Black people, but why that's less important than some of the other truths about Black poverty, crime, and violence to understand. **And share these conversations with your kids.** You got this.

CHAPTER 14

The Extra Stuff Black Women Go Through

listen

Stacey Abrams. We see her as a hero, and truly, a key figure in not only the 2020 elections but in upholding democracy in the United States.

But if you were in Georgia in 2018 during her gubernatorial campaign (yes, the one with all the actual voter suppression), you would have surely heard someone, many someones, describe her as an "angry black woman." And not loudly, but in whispers on the side—which is, as we know, the most damaging way to disparage someone. Because then it's seen as true.

According to online magazine *The Root*, the team working for Stacey Evans (Abrams's Democractic opposition, who also happens to be a White, married, thirty-nine-year-old state representative from Smyrna, Georgia) spread rumors of Abrams being an "angry black woman" and a lesbian in order to convince voters that she wasn't worthy of the office of governor. Because, after all, who wants an "angry black woman" running the state of Georgia? What's worse than that?

Well, what's worse than that is this: It worked.

learn

Nasty. Mad. Angry.

When you hear those words, who do you picture?

Domineering. Aggressive. Threatening. Loud.

Who do you picture now?

Although it will likely surprise you the way it does us, lots of people have pictured Kamala Harris, Serena Williams, Stacey Abrams, and Michelle Obama that way. There's a reason for it: The above terms have been used repeatedly to describe each of those women within the last five years by White people who are invoking one or both of two long-held White supremacist stereotypes of Black women—the "angry Black woman" and the "mammy."

The "angry black woman" stereotype has been around for close to two hundred years now. It comes from minstrel shows in the 1800s, which included comedy sketches and variety acts and mocked Black people. In particular, notes Blair Kelley, an associate professor of history at North Carolina State University, in an article for the BBC website by Rita Prasad, "[B]lack women were often played by overweight White men who painted their faces Black and donned fat suits 'to make them look less than human, unfeminine, ugly.'" These "women" would scream and fight and be angry with the men in these skits, thereby making them seem irrationally angry with regard to everything, and everyone, else.

In the 1930s, *Amos 'n' Andy*, a radio sketch comedy series started in Harlem featuring White actors with minstrel show experience, further pushed this stereotype by creating a "Black" female character named Sapphire Stevens, whose role was to be angry and irrational. And, as America moved further into Jim Crow laws, popular culture continued to uphold this stereotype of "sassy mammies" and "Sapphires," Kelley says, to portray "Black women with iron fists, yelling at everyone from children to White men."

So while this isn't a new stereotype, it's one that is still thrown in the face of any Black woman who dares to raise her voice. That has to be exhausting. And infuriating. Prasad also spoke to Robin Boylorn, an intercultural communications professor at the University of Alabama, who rightfully stated: "Black women should be celebrated for not being completely consumed by anger."

Boylorn continued, "Men are allowed to be angry as a performance of masculinity. White women are allowed to be angry as a clarion call. So Black women should be encouraged to express their anger as well, particularly in the face of injustice." Sit with that for a moment.

How do you view men or boys, of any color, who are angry? How do you view White women, or White girls, who express anger? Do you view them any differently than Black women or Black girls who are angry?

Let's switch gears and address another Black female trope that has been around for so long, to this day many people have never thought twice about it. Have you ever bought an Aunt Jemima product? Do you know the history of the "mammy" figure on the box?

Reporter Layla Eplett writes in an article for *Scientific American* that Aunt Jemima's pancake mix was created in 1889 "when two [White] speculators, Chris Rutt and Charles Underwood, bought a bankrupt flour mill. They invented the pancake mixture in hopes of creating a demand for their flour. Initially, it was simply called 'Self-Rising Pancake Flour' but as Maurice Manring, author of *Slave in a Box: The Strange Career of Aunt Jemima* explains, Rutt decided to rename the flour after attending a minstrel show. 'Old Aunt Jemima' was originally a song that was sung by field slaves, then later adapted and performed thousands of times at minstrel shows. When Rutt saw Peter Baker dance and perform as Aunt Jemima wearing an apron, bandana, and Blackface at one of these shows, he decided to name his flour mix after the woman featured in the song."

The way that the pancake mix was originally marketed to White housewives was particularly racist. For his story and the title of his book, as you saw above, Manring described Aunt Jemima as a "slave in a box." Why did Manring use this provocative phrase? "The reason I call her a 'slave in a box' is largely because of the way the product was advertised to presumably White housewives and that is because it drew heavily on the themes of plantation slavery and on the servant who had the time and the ability to do things you don't feel competent to do yourself. And who, by the way, loved doing it for you."

In spite of the fact that Aunt Jemima has been stirring controversy as a symbol of racist ideology since just a few years after her invention in the nineteenth century, she was a common household figure for over 130 years. If you're familiar with the book and especially the movie *Gone with the Wind*, you know that the concept of the mammy and the image it represents of Black women in happy servitude has lived strong in the media through generations. And for just as long, this subservient trope of a servant or slave "yes ma'am"-ing her way through one chore at a time, all for the benefit of the White female slave or home owner, has been greatly hurtful to Black women.

So you can understand why, thankfully, the offensive logo was finally removed from Quaker Oats packaging after George Floyd was murdered in the summer of 2020. But the damage to how we view Black women, and the reinforcing of the Black mammy stereotype as one that is taking care of White people—and does not need to be taken care of herself—has already been done in so many ways.

Oregon-based ob-gyn Dr. Jennifer Lincoln released a TikTok video in 2020 that talked about the differences in care between Black and White patients. The video went viral because it touched on a particularly important and sensitive issue: the disparate treatment that Black women receive in areas like maternal healthcare. Even Serena Williams, who was the number-one-ranked women's tennis player in the world at the time of giving birth to her daughter, almost died in the maternity ward because her voice was silenced as to her own medical needs.

In the video, Lincoln states that "a 2016 study showed that 50 percent of medical students and residents who were studied believed that Black people couldn't feel pain the same way because they had thicker skin or their nerves didn't work the same way." If that sounds ridiculous to you, it should. But it likely influences how doctors perceive pain management—and other medical care—for Black people.

Racist tropes. Medical misinformation. And that's just the tip of the iceberg of issues that you have to navigate as you move through American society if you're a Black woman. There's also: being careful to dress in colorful, trendy clothes when you go jogging in your predominantly White neighborhood and making sure to notify several friends of your exact jogging route in case you don't come back. Having your name mispronounced ("Kama-la-la-la") on local or national stages. Being called "Breonna" by several

Congressmen when you show up in Congress for your freshman orientation wearing a "Breonna Taylor" mask. Being forgotten if you are a Black woman and murdered by the police, without the months of media coverage and outrage that would accompany your death if you were White.

> **MICROAGGRESSION: Dismissing a Black woman as being "too angry"**

We could go on, but you get the point (all true examples, by the way). Now that you know that, by virtue of being both Black and female, Black women are often marginalized on two fronts, their voices left unheard because of racism and sexism—how do you feel when you hear the words "angry Black woman"?

It's easier to fit Black women neatly into a stereotypical box than to address the issues of hearing and seeing individuals in all their humanity. And if you're looking at how your kids are going to be internalizing those stereotypes—it's time to break the cycle. Right now.

act ━━━━━━━━━━━━━━━━━━━━━━━━━━ 📣

So how do you change a stereotype? First, and this is an important one—widen your circle of friends. **It's not enough to have one Black friend—and it sure isn't enough to have no Black friends.** We understand that due to the way neighborhoods are composed of people of the same race, this may not be an organic thing. Maybe your kids go to a predominantly White independent (private) school, or you live in an all-White neighborhood, or you work in a place where it's largely White people.

This means that this may not be easy. **But, like everything else in this book, it can happen in small steps; it just needs to be intentional, and considered often.**

Find organizations in your community, or spaces, that draw a more diverse crowd. Maybe it's finding an organization that's somewhere else that you can connect with virtually. Maybe it's trying out new activities with your kids. Maybe it's even going as far as considering a switch in neighborhoods, or schools, to expose your children to Black kids in a way that is going to profoundly affect how they view Black people. (More on that one in the next chapter.) **But, most importantly, it's you being intentional about who is in your friend group, who is in the group of people that you have around your children. Because remember—you can't be who you can't see.** If you only have White friends, that remains your "normal," and if you have kids, they'll accept it as normal, too. And they're going to lose out on the benefits of having conversations with Black girls, and Black women, who can show them that those stereotypes are just that—hateful, racist stereotypes that are intended to keep White supremacy fully in place.

MICROAGGRESSION: Mispronouncing someone's name, accidentally or on purpose, because "it sounds different"

Pay attention also to whose voices you are listening to when it comes to expressions of what it means to be a woman. Are you reading books by Black female authors? Are you watching shows written by Black women? Are you listening to podcasts hosted by Black women? None of these take a lot of extra time—but, when done intentionally, they will shift your thinking and thought patterns. And the same goes for your kids. There are books, music, and media out there that will encourage kids to consider how they view people. A special note to the moms who are raising daughters: Exposing your daughters to the beauty and strength that Black women and girls embody will enable them to be accomplices and allies for *all* women down the road.

As best friends Aminatou Sow and Ann Friedman wrote in their book, *Big Friendship*, genuine friendship requires honest dialogue across color lines. "There is no way to be intimately close with people if you refuse to engage in the truth of how the world is organized," Sow said in an interview with the *New York Times*. This means that, especially for those of us who are new to conversations about race, putting in all of the internal and external work we've talked about in this book so far helps us set the foundation to be able to develop a true, authentic friendship across racial lines.

Let's break the system—together.

P.S. One last note about names. Names are so important. Please, please do not shy away from the names that seem "hard" to you. As Misasha can personally attest to, using someone's name helps them feel seen. If you're not sure about someone's name, simply ask, "I love your name. How do you pronounce it?" **Then say her name**. Don't leave someone out or mispronounce someone's name out of fear on your part. In some ways, it's a microaggression. And also, a denial of her humanity. Model this behavior for your kids. Use people's names and show your kids how to do the same.

CHAPTER 15

School Choice, Buying, and Nice White Parents

listen

In the summer of 2020, the *New York Times* released a six-episode podcast called *Nice White Parents*. Prior to the first episode even being released, we noticed that there were a number of one-star reviews on Apple Podcasts. If the series was on your radar, you're probably aware of what some of those reviews said: *racist title, this isn't the issue, why blame White parents, this is some liberal B.S.* In other words, White fragility (see page 27 for a discussion about that).

The feelings that the title of this podcast stirred up among many White parents are not new. Many parents, and so many that we've personally spoken to, want equity in schools. They want the opportunities in every school and classroom not to be linked to race or class but to really enable all kids to succeed in a learning environment. We hear you.

But how many of us live in predominantly White neighborhoods? Send our kids to predominantly White public schools or predominantly White independent schools, especially if we are White ourselves? Continue to buy houses in these areas where our White friends live because it's in a "good school district"?

How do we get to an equitable school system if we, or if White parents in general, are not willing to be the people stepping up to force change through? Ironically—or perhaps not—that was the subject of *Nice White Parents*. People wanted desegregated schools with equal opportunities—but when push came to shove, they didn't want their kids going there, or they didn't want those schools to replace their "nice" neighborhood schools. And for the few parents who were motivated to really, intentionally push through that change? They were met with resistance on all levels, which weakened their internal resolve in the end. And the status quo remains.

How did we get to this status quo in the first place, though, when we thought We the People have had the American Dream firmly in the forefront of our minds for so long, even more so for our children? Hopefully, if you've made it this far in the book, you're beginning to see all of the ways that systemic racism impacts every facet of our society—education included. And if you read the chapter about gangs (page 131), which highlighted how White flight made segregated areas even more segregated, you probably have an idea of how schools in different neighborhoods could look very, very different.

As we were writing this book, the sixtieth anniversary of six-year-old Ruby Bridges walking into an all-White school in Mississippi took place. **It's only been sixty years since school desegregation was really enforced in this country,** and even then, much of that enforcement was begrudging acceptance at best, active disregard for and blocking at worst. Many of our parents were born in a time when segregation was still firmly the law of the land. In other words, this isn't history. These are scenarios that are happening in our lifetimes.

learn ⎯⎯⎯⎯⎯⎯⎯⎯⎯⎯⎯⎯⎯⎯⎯ 📖

Let's back up a little. On May 17, 1954, the Supreme Court decided in the landmark *Brown v. Board of Education* case that segregation in public schools constituted unequal treatment and was therefore unlawful. For White southerners (and probably some White north-erners as well), this decision attacked White supremacy at its core, because it was suggesting that, on some level, Black and White children were equal. They channeled their anger and racism into a strategy called "massive resistance," which was really a fancy term for "doing everything lawful—and unlawful—that we can to stop this desegregation thing from happening." Some areas, like Prince Edward County in Virginia, closed its entire public school system rather than integrate their schools.

You may have heard of some of the cases of resistance, like the Little Rock Nine in Arkansas, who were the first nine Black students to enroll in the all-White Little Rock Central High School, and who faced such a level of hostility and threats that President Eisenhower had to call in the military to help protect these students.

But what you may not have heard is what went on outside of news coverage. Historian Sonya Ramsey writes, "While [the Little Rock Nine] case garnered national attention, most southern school officials quietly developed their own plans to delay or deny the implementation of desegregation, including grade-per-year plans, transfer plans, and school closings. In addition, school boards also funneled money and supplies to existing facilities and constructed new Black schools to dispute claims that they were underfunded and quell the desire for integration. When this strategy failed and federal court orders forced school districts to develop new desegregation plans, Black teachers faced massive job losses as White school boards closed Black schools. African American principals, who once held one of the most powerful and prestigious positions within African American communities, also received demotions or lost their jobs as their schools were eliminated."

With the Civil Rights Act, withholding of government funding for schools without desegregation, further court cases, and the Cold War, America's public schools looked as if they were being pushed towards a future that included all children at the same schools. But that didn't account for how the government also aided White flight, both physically and financially, at that exact same time.

As discussed in prior chapters, the GI Bill and the availability of Federal Housing Association (FHA) mortgages helped create a White middle class that was largely based in the suburbs—but barred Black families from the same advantages. Suburbs became a status symbol for White people—and that included the creation of new neighborhood schools in these predominantly White suburbs.

Black families, however, were largely stuck in the cities, in the now older and fewer schools, with less access to supplies and teachers but with more crowded classrooms and all of the obstacles that remained.

Even with desegregation having been legally achieved, the physical segregation of neighborhoods presented a barrier to actually changing any policies. That's where busing came in. In *Swann v. Charlotte Mecklenburg County Board of Education*, the Supreme Court ruled in 1971 that this was the most feasible way to achieve desegregation—as busing would take children to schools outside their own segregated neighborhoods. It should be noted, however, that "school systems in rural areas had transported White students out of their neighborhoods to attend school for decades, while Black students were sometimes denied access to public school transportation." So busing wasn't new. But when it was ruled that all kids were potentially going to be bused—that wasn't okay.

Why? Well, here is perhaps the crux of the problem. Ramsey continues, "Although studies reflected that a majority of White parents did not object to Black students attending school with their children, **they drew the line when it came time for their children to attend schools in what they deemed [to be] unsafe Black neighborhoods.**" Also, if you were wealthy and White, you had options that didn't include busing. So, in true American fashion, antibusing protests started, and independent schools provided an option for parents to get around the busing mandate, especially in increasingly White suburbia.

When people leave, so does money. Suburban areas "experienced more economic development as urban areas lost some of their tax base." And busing didn't ease racial tensions—far from it. Racist epithets were hurled at Black students on buses in southern and northern cities alike, for example Detroit and Boston, often from White mothers (remember little Antonio in Chapter 9)?

And indeed, White mothers often were the loudest adversaries of busing. A 1970s election advertisement for Governor Claude Kirk of Florida featured three White mothers talking about how they weren't going to send their White daughters on buses to school when there were perfectly good schools in their own neighborhoods. It was also Florida where activists believed that the outcome of busing would be interracial marriages and mixed-race children, and they therefore opposed busing by opposing "race mixing" of any kind. As a poem written by Betty Laine Larsen at the time asks, "Will the time ever come when the pit of my soul / Won't cringe in sheer agony / As Black and White inter-breed to produce / A 'gray society?'"

Yes. That's the end of an actual poem. And the poem echoes the real, stated fears and hostility of a lot of other White women at the time, not just Betty's.

The impact on Black families wasn't just through racial epithets. It was through logistics as well. Black children were being bused across town, and because of the bus schedule were not participating in any pre- or post-school activities. Few Black parents were attending PTA meetings or other school events due to distance. Education quality suffered because, up until that point, the bused kids and the local kids had been educated at different levels. White parents began looking for private schools or new, suburban neighborhoods, even in "liberal" areas like Washington, D.C. And many believed that these changes were not due to racism, they were due to the fact that busing didn't work. We think both can be true.

And the segregation has endured.

According to the Brookings Institute, the average White student's public school had a Black enrollment of about 10 percent in 2010, which was roughly the same as in 1980. The average Black student's public school actually had less White enrollment in 2010 than in 1980, partly due to the growth of Hispanic students in the school age population in this thirty-year period, and the related decline in the White population.

In this thirty-year period, we've also had a number of policies such as No Child Left Behind ("NCLB") and Race to the Top, as well as numerous court cases, that effectively encourage students and their families to "choose" to leave traditional public school education for other options, be it charter schools, private schools, homeschooling, or voucher programs. Choice sounds great, but the effect isn't. Many argue that school choice is perpetuating racism, as it's more often than not wealthier White families who make the choice to opt out, and underrepresented families, in particular Black families, who are poor and have been stuck in the inner-city areas for generations, who are left behind. It highlights the stark realities of the link between class and race in our country, and the cycles that are hard to break.

act ━━━━━━━━━━━━━━━━━━━━━━━━━ 📢

So what can you do if you want your kids to be in a diverse school environment? **We like to start by asking questions.** Ask questions of your current school, especially if it's an independent one (as you really are the customer there!), or within the PTA for a public school. Find out how they bring students in and how they treat students while they are there.

Next? **Ask yourself what is truly important to you and your family, in terms of values and the diversity that you'd like to see in the spheres that you move in.** Maybe your neighborhood isn't diverse, and you're not able or don't want to move to a more integrated neighborhood (put a pin in that—we'll circle back to that in a moment). But maybe you can create groups that are diverse where you are, including ones that your kids are involved in. It comes back, fundamentally, to the community—who the community supports, and how. Make sure that your community reflects your values, and not the opposite.

On the school choice issue, you may want to ask yourself (and other parents) some of the harder questions like, if an independent school may be better for my child academically, what's the trade-off in terms of diverse access to race and socioeconomics? How do I want my child's peer group to look? What have other parents done when faced with the same questions, and why? Is there a way within my community to achieve all of these goals; how have other parents tackled this?

Let's circle back as promised to those of you who feel uncertain about moving or putting your kids in a public school for the sake of a diverse experience—is it because you think that those neighborhoods or schools are "less safe"? If so, ask yourself if that is the problem of the kids and parents in that neighborhood or school, or if there is something you can do to foster change? **Look again for the mutual aid networks in those communities and find ways that you—and your kids—can contribute.**

If you're happy with the school your kids are in, you can still take new actions to promote diversity and anti-racism and to give back to those in your community who may need help. Check with your school principal to see if there's a need for a food pantry for children to take food home to eat over the weekend. Make sure that each classroom at your child's school is stocked with books featuring diverse characters doing regular, everyday things—so that kids can see and read about people who look different than they do, yet still do the exact same things that they do. Check to see if there are affinity groups—groups centered around people who are not in the majority and have concerns that often go unheard for lack of representation—at your kid's school and find ways you can support them. Show up at school and support events that focus on diversity, and make sure that the PTA for your kids' schools (or the administration, or both) are supporting diversity education and racial literacy for their teachers, staff, parents, and school communities. Make sure that critical thinking is being taught, starting early on, so that kids are able to parse through what they've been told as they focus on helping others.

Start breaking those cycles of disinterest and detachment for "other people's problems" through involvement in whatever way you can. But do this intentionally, and often. Because remember that there are many kids who wish for half the shot that your kids have, and those will be the kids that your kids will grow up with—together, or not.

CHAPTER 16

Rooting for Everybody Black

listen ─────────────────────────────────────

"You do know why our numbers changed, right? It's because you got rid of your locs."

This wasn't the response that Eric was expecting, but it didn't surprise him. For years, sales and business had been the same at his company—and then suddenly there was an uptick. He didn't immediately put the two things together. You see, Eric is a Black man, who until recently had locs—a very "Black" hairstyle.

A brief but important explanation: You might know locs as "dreadlocks." We call them "locs" because, as noted by Lori L. Tharps, hair historian and coauthor of *Hair Story: Untangling the Roots of Black Hair in America*, "the modern understanding of dreadlocks is that the British, who were fighting Kenyan warriors (during colonialism in the late 19th century), came across the warriors' locs and found them 'dreadful,' thus coining the term 'dreadlocks.'" Once we learned this, we consciously changed how we refer to this hairstyle, and hope you will too.

Back to Eric. He cut off his locs. Business got better. Now, the two things might not be correlated—but we think they are. In cutting off his locs, he became suddenly less "Black" in a predominantly

White neighborhood, selling to a predominantly White clientele. He's suddenly less threatening. More acceptable.

Is that what it takes? For Black people to be more "White," in order to compete? We don't think it should. Yet at the same time, there are so many White-owned businesses out there, and so few Black-owned businesses, that it seems like business in America is, by default, SO White.

learn————————————————————📖

Why aren't there more Black-owned businesses in the first place?

Wealth. Specifically, the lack of wealth in the Black community. As we write this book, the U.S. is coming off another census year and still tabulating, but the most recent Census Bureau data that we've seen shows a typical Black household having just 6 percent of the wealth of the typical White household. In 2011, the median White household had $111,146 in wealth holdings, compared with just $7,113 for the median Black household.

MICROAGGRESSION: Reaching to touch a Black person's hair without permission

We know one reason for this wealth gap—years and generations of slavery, which wiped out all wealth holdings for Black families. Yet, even now, decades post-slavery, this wealth gap exists. A Brookings Institute article quotes economists Darrick Hamilton and Sandy Darity as concluding that inheritances and other inter-generational transfers "account for more of the racial wealth gap than any other demographic and socioeconomic indicators."

Think about that for a second. Inheritance may be something that many White families count on, directly or indirectly, as they consider the transfer of wealth from generation to generation. However, Black American families largely had all familial wealth wiped out with slavery. They basically started with nothing from the end of the Civil War—which didn't end all that long ago. How much wealth can you really build in 150 years, when you start with no property, no opportunities for education, no governmental support, no jobs, and laws in place that prevent you from even getting a foothold from which to start building said wealth?

> **MICROAGGRESSION: Assuming a person of color working in a store isn't the owner**

Maybe you're thinking, I'm not getting an inheritance but I work hard so that's how I can afford to spend money how I want. We agree that in an ideal world, everyone would be able to do the same. However, racism plays a part in disparate outcomes in the labor market—through employment discrimination, geographic barriers to jobs, and differing levels of social capital. According to a 2015 Forbes report, the typical White family earns $50,400 a year, while the typical Black family earns $32,048.

But here's where we see a huge gap: The wealth return to one dollar of income is almost more important than income itself as a measure—in other words, what you're able to save (versus what you absolutely need to spend) and the return you earn on that savings. According to Forbes, a White family will typically see a return of $19.51 for each dollar earned, while a Black family will see only $4.80 in return (four times less return per dollar). And of course, that growth becomes exponential over generations.

It's not just income that's a measure of wealth, though. There's also homeownership, which is a key indicator of wealth, and one where racism also has a severe impact. Whereas 73 percent of White Americans own a home, only 45 percent of Black Americans do. The disparity persists in the value of those homes as well: the median White house is worth $85,000; the median Black house is worth $50,000.

While Chapters 2 (page 29), 13 (page 131), and 15 (page 151) gave us some insight into why the location of these homes might vary, and why therefore the home values might vary (remember the blockbusting strategy described on page 135), the federal government played a distinct role in kicking off this home-value disparity.

The 1934 National Housing Act effectively redlined (see page 32) Black neighborhoods, marking them as credit risks and refusing to invest in them, through mortgages or otherwise. Although this was considered illegal by the 1960s, the damage was already done. The neighborhoods largely populated to that point by people of color, and in particular Black Americans, were poorer, lacked infrastructure, and were considered less desirable.

That's not to say that discriminatory lending doesn't exist today—it definitely does. As Forbes notes: "Mortgages obtained by households of color tend to have higher interest rates. Even as recently as 2012, Wells Fargo admitted it had steered Black and Latino households into subprime mortgages but had offered White borrowers with similar credit profiles prime mortgages." In other words, this isn't a problem that's in the past. It continues to define how wealth is amassed in this country, and how it's so much harder to do that when you're Black due to systemic obstacles.

There's one last piece to this puzzle that we need to discuss: education. In Chapter 15 (page 151), we broke down how desegregation and school choice have contributed to the continuing disparity in education for Black people in this country. While we were focused on primary and secondary education in that chapter, it's not a stretch to link early and secondary education with higher education. And, not surprisingly, the numbers there highlight another institutional problem.

Not having a college degree can be a barrier to better-paying jobs. However, in 2011, 34 percent of Whites graduated from a four-year college compared to just 20 percent of Black people. One large barrier to college attendance? Student loans. The ability to pay that debt back—or rather, the inability to do so—is often a total barrier to Black higher education, which is why the argument to forgive student loans is a key one to pay attention to, as this may help address this racial barrier to higher education.

Even if you're able to fund the tuition and graduate from that four-year college, is the investment really worth it, if you're Black? The surprising answer is: not really. The lifetime return on investment for completing a four-year college degree for a White family at the median income level is $55,869. For a Black family? $4,896. Yes. Less than $5,000. Why is that the case? Two reasons: Black students take on larger amounts of debt for higher education, and then face discrimination in the workplace once they have finally earned that degree. And it starts even earlier—remember our history of redlining (see page 32)? Black children who grow up in certain areas often go to primary and secondary schools with fewer resources, which affects higher education preparedness. So—the path to higher education is long, debt-filled, and riddled with obstacles. By the time a young Black person is ready to enter the workforce, they're starting out behind. Given all that, who would want to go into serious debt for a $5,000 return on investment? Not many of us, I'm guessing.

act

So how do we change this pattern? How do we make things more equitable for our children's generation? **Perhaps the easiest way to break these patterns here is to shop at Black-owned businesses.** In order to have and build generational wealth, we need to help get money into the Black communities. Now, more than ever, companies and organizations have made it easier to look for Black-owned businesses. On Etsy. Through bloggers. A Google search. No more excuses.

You may be reading this right after you filled your Amazon cart, because you have Prime two-day shipping and you forgot that your kid needs an art project finished by basically yesterday—we get it, we know the feeling. But we're going to challenge you to do this: **Be more intentional about who you shop with.** It's not easy and there's probably not an app for that, but you are voting with your wallet. You are using your purchasing power to level the playing field, so that your children will have more choices when it's their turn to be the primary purchasers of goods and services. In putting your dollars into Black communities, you'll be helping to support not only this generation of Black entrepreneurs, but future ones as well. Some places that we love as starting points for Black-owned businesses are Shoppe Black, Dough, Buy from a Black Woman Directory, and WeBuyBlack. A quick Google search can point you to local Black-owned businesses in your area that you may not know about and can visit. Try another search to find and see how you can support local Black artisans, makers, and doers in your very own backyard.

Again, no excuses. It might take longer. It might not be two-day free shipping. But you'll be changing the course of your kids' generation, one purchase at a time, because you will be giving Black entrepreneurs, and others who support the Black community, a chance at building generational wealth. And to us, that's worth a whole lot more than free shipping.

On Being a Non-Black Person of Color in America

SECTION III

CHAPTER 17

The Dangers of the "China Flu"

Most studies and articles on racism in the United States focus on Black Americans. Given the history of slavery in this country, this focus isn't altogether surprising. In addition to the slow and complex process of dismantling the structural and institutional policies that have long perpetuated discrimination and inequity against Black people in our country, there is obviously still a lot of work to be done to address interpersonal hatred and misunderstanding.

However, we'd be leaving a huge hole in the conversation if we didn't address the racism that is directed toward non-Black people of color in the U.S. While we dive into issues facing specific minority groups in this and the following chapters, the crucially important bottom line we will keep emphasizing is the need to stop seeing people as stereotypes and start seeing them as individuals. To be sure, humans tend to be drawn to the easiest way of seeing things; we put things into categories to make sense of a complex world, and define people and things around us by their broadest characteristics. This is why we need to remain aware of both the automatic and the subtle ways we put labels on people, and the dangers of that.

Here are two examples.

Researchers had students in an elementary school classroom take intelligence pre-tests; the researchers then told the teachers which students had scored in the top 20 percent and were expected to show "unusual potential for intellectual growth" and bloom within the next year. In reality, these students were selected randomly with no relation to their actual performance on the test. When the researchers followed up less than a year later, they found that the students who had been identified as bloomers scored significantly higher than the students who hadn't been identified. Even though they had all had the same baseline, the teachers had fostered the development of those bloomers differently over the course of the school year, and in fact created a self-fulfilling prophecy. The kids who were labeled as smart, even though they were just the same as others, were treated as such and actually became smarter.

> *"When we expect certain behaviors of others,*
> *we are likely to act in ways that make the*
> *expected behavior more likely to occur."*
> (ROSENTHAL AND BABAD, 1985)

In another study, researchers showed participants a video of a fourth-grade girl named Hannah taking an academic test, and they made sure that her performance was inconsistent, so participants wouldn't get a clear sense of her ability from the test alone. They showed some participants videos of Hannah playing in a low-income housing area and told them that her parents only had high-school educations and worked as a meat packer and seamstress; for others, they showed Hannah playing in a tree-lined park with a suburban model school, and indicated that her parents were college graduates and had careers as lawyers and writers. The participants imposed their own beliefs of stereotypes onto Hannah —those who saw her in the lower socioeconomic setting graded her as performing below grade level, while those who saw her as middle class graded her as above grade level.

Imagine how our beliefs about underrepresented groups like Asians, Latinx, Indigenous people, and immigrants might play into our views and treatment of individuals. Often without realizing it, we reduce people to fit into a small, preconceived range of characteristics and behavior, and assume that they all share some innate qualities. The consequence of sitting with our assumptions and applying labels is that we abandon our better nature to feel and appreciate individuality, for a kind of self-fulfilling view that only lets us see what we want to see, and in the process, our views may impact how we interact with people from those groups.

> **MICROAGGRESSION: Saying, "You aren't like the other Black/Hispanic/Asian/Indigenous people I know."**

We give much credit to the individualism inherent in White success in America—that is to say, when a White person succeeds, in our culture it is assumed it's because of that person's self-determination and abilities. But because of the many labels and messages heaped upon and around Black people and non-Black people of color, that assumed respect is often not equally conferred. We have to stay aware and give the same recognition of achievement and success to every non-White individual too—AND just as importantly, acknowledge the additional struggles they have had to overcome based on their ethnic identity, to get to where they have up to this point. Let's dive in, starting with current events: how dangerous it gets if we illogically blame a group of people for diseases that spread around the world, instead of looking at individual cases and sub-groups more specifically.

You remember the early days of that unknown virus that arrived in 2019 and ravaged the population of the globe that year and for all of 2020 and beyond. Along with upheaval everywhere, wearing masks suddenly became a thing that people did. We were dancing around each other, trying to eyeball a six-foot distance, like we all had contagious pathogens; Sara remembers sneezing in the line at the supermarket, and holding her hands up, proclaiming, "It's not COVID!" She heard some awkward chuckles. It was a frightening and uncomfortable time for everybody.

Unfortunately, for people of Asian descent, the virus carried another set of threats.

Before COVID hit our shores in 2019, the FBI reported that victims of anti-Asian bias made up 4.3 percent of total hate crimes in the United States. As a target, Asians were not high on the list. However, between 2019 and 2020 in New York City, a fairly diverse city by any measure, hate crimes confirmed by the NYPD against Asians increased by 2300 percent. That's stunning.

In addition to straight-up violence, there also was a tremendous uptick in verbal harassment, including racial slurs, name calling, and profanities, and an increase in shunning, meaning the deliberate avoidance of Asian American and Pacific Islanders (AAPIs) because of their race. The National Report from Stop AAPI Hate recorded 6,603 incident reports from March 19, 2020 to March 31, 2021, with the number increasing significantly over time; these included firsthand accounts of hurtful incidents against Asian people since COVID-19 hit our shores:

- "I'm a healthcare worker. I saw a maskless man sit across from me on the subway. I moved to the other side of the train car and he followed. He spat and coughed on the subway while yelling racial slurs. No one stood up for me." (New York, NY)

- "I was in line at the pharmacy when a woman approached me and sprayed Lysol all over me. She was yelling out, 'You're the infection. Go home. We don't want you here!' I was in shock and cried as I left the building. No one came to my help." (Marietta, GA)

- "I got into the elevator, mask on, so I could get my mail from the lobby. The elevator opened on the fourth floor and this unmasked white woman yelled 'OH HELL NO' when she saw me. The elevator door opened on the first floor and she gets out of the elevator and looks me up and down and goes, 'You f**king Chinese people, you're not going to get away with this, we're going to get you.'" (Portland, OR)

Imagine: You're an American. You have physical characteristics that show your heritage—characteristics you cannot control, characteristics that you were born with—and because of a disease that's just as out of your control, you're being verbally assaulted and shunned by people in your community. The incidents aren't just targeted at adults either; this sort of stuff is happening to kids too. According to Manjusha Kulkarni, the executive director of A3PCON, "We are currently providing support to a child who had to go to the emergency room after he was assaulted and accused by bullies of having the coronavirus, and so that tells us we may need to work with schools to address shunning and school bullying."

Where did this hatred come from?

For starters, President Trump's racially insensitive language. He repeatedly referred to COVID-19 as the "kung flu" or "China virus," even reportedly crossing out the word "corona" in his official speech notes and replacing it with "Chinese." He certainly didn't take a stand against hatred and discrimination against Asian people. To the contrary, the phrases he used were then echoed by other members of the media and administration. Some would say—we say—that language like that further fans the flames of hatred and discrimination. Words matter. According to a report from the Asian Pacific Policy & Planning Council, over 25 percent included some use of the word "China" or "Chinese" during the altercation; swearing and demeaning individuals; telling people to "go back to where they came from"; or indicating that the victim of the assault was responsible for the virus. Keep in mind, people didn't take time to confirm whether that person of Asian descent was in fact Chinese; anyone who looked Asian was a potential target, regardless of what country they were from or descended from. That sort of abuse can have serious long-term impact and may cause permanent psychological trauma such as PTSD, anxiety, and depression to those who are targeted.

learn

We know we don't need to say this, but why not say it again: It's NOT the China flu; it's COVID-19, which is caused by SARS-CoV-2. It's important for all of us to pause and think about the fact that we have a long history of associating diseases with certain countries and communities, which has led to discrimination based on people's race or ethnicity. This pattern of pointing fingers has hurt efforts to respond effectively to public health crises, and also given us a misleading understanding of the history of infectious diseases and how they spread.

In the 1850s, for example, the New York Marine Hospital on Staten Island quarantined immigrants who arrived with diseases like smallpox, cholera, and typhus. At that time, some people referred to cholera as the "Irish disease," and blamed Irish and Jewish people for yellow fever. Anti-immigrant sentiment was compounded by fear, and instead of changing the conditions that spread them (like reducing the number of immigrants packed below deck during their travels to the United States, which created a scenario ripe for transmission) and allowing medical professionals to focus on curing these diseases, angry locals burned the New York Marine Hospital to the ground. Nobody was held accountable, as the facility was deemed a danger to the community. Quarantining individuals—immigrants—by force, as opposed to in a more ethical manner, was also of questionable effectiveness. But it leads us to wonder, would people who were considered "Americans," as opposed to immigrants, have been forced to quarantine?

Around the same time on the other side of the country in California, Chinese immigrants were being unjustly blamed for economic problems in the country (even though they made up only .002 percent of the population), and also for epidemics like cholera and smallpox. These forces led to the Chinese Exclusion Act of 1882, which was the first time there was *any* federal law about immigration—effectively limiting all immigration from China (students and diplomats were excepted) and not allowing Chinese residents to become naturalized citizens. Even under these restrictions, after which Chinese people were forced to carry around certificates of residence to prove that they'd entered the United States legally, Chinese people continued to be blamed for other epidemics. When, in 1900, a Chinese immigrant living in Chinatown in San Francisco was found through autopsy to have died of the bubonic plague, the fear and accusations kicked up again. And while White people who had visited Chinatown during that time were not quarantined, immigrants and Chinese Americans in the district were strictly quarantined. What does this say about our country's selective, race-based policies when it comes to protecting people against diseases that do not discriminate based on race?

In another example, the 1918 "Spanish flu"—the one that killed many millions of people and infected 40 percent of the world—actually did not start in Spain (where it was known as the "French flu"). In fact, we still don't definitively know where it started—it could've been in France, China, Britain, or even Kansas in the United States. The only reason that pandemic got the nickname Spanish flu is because while other countries suppressed reporting on the flu to keep morale up during World War I, the Spanish media freely reported on all the details. When people could only get news about the outbreak from Spanish sources, they assumed that was where it began. But contrary to its nickname, some scientists surmise that the so-called Spanish flu was actually a bird flu that may have started on a pig farm in Kansas, where a soldier on a military base became the first case ever recorded of that deadly flu, one that unleashed a mutated virus that humans had never developed immunity for before. Many Americans *still* believe the outbreak started in Spain, so how would finding out that it started in the U.S. change our view of that pandemic? And what parallels exist between historic pandemics with the most recent pandemic that was first linked to a local seafood market in Wuhan, China in 2019, and subsequently spread across the world?

> MICROAGGRESSION: Asking a person if they are here legally, or assuming they're not

We may have finally learned from history: This virus and its disease were notably *not* named for its location or ethnic origins. Dr. Steve Berger, cofounder of Gideon, an app targeted to healthcare professionals, notes that "the naming of a pathogen for the region it was discovered in can be stigmatizing and have geopolitical ramifications. The World Health Organization made a point to exclude the terms 'Wuhan' and 'China' when naming the current pandemic disease." Instead, they focused on pathology: coronaviruses (CoVs) are so named because they have crownlike (*corona* in Latin) spikey projections that stick out from their surface when examined under an electron microscope.

The 2019 pandemic is therefore referred to in this way: SARS-CoV-2 (severe acute respiratory syndrome coronavirus 2) is the name of the virus that causes the disease known as COVID-19 (coronavirus disease of 2019). The terminology is parallel to that of the human immunodeficiency virus (HIV) that causes the disease acquired immunodeficiency syndrome (AIDS). The virus is the cause, the disease is the result.

Just like other recent SARS-CoV epidemics (in 2003 and 2012), the 2019 virus appears to have thrived by moving from animals to humans. When scientists looked into the 2019 virus's genome, it showed considerable similarities to a coronavirus found in a bat, and they speculate that there was an intermediary animal (currently suspected to be a pangolin) that then infected humans. Because they haven't found the specific animals infected from that initial site, though, there is no definitive proof of the line of transmission in 2019.

That said, scientists call a harmful germ that spreads from animals to people a zoonoses (or zoonotic disease), and these are not all that rare. The CDC says that "approximately 60 percent of known infectious diseases in people, such as rabies, ringworm, and salmonellosis, are transmitted from animals." Typically, zoonotic diseases spread when a person comes into direct contact with the infected animal; has indirect contact with the animal's habitat or surfaces that have been contaminated with their germs; eats food or drinks water that's become contaminated with feces from the infected animal; or is bitten by an insect that carries the germs. Suffice it to say, unlike some of the stories suggesting that some Chinese person ate a bat and that started this whole pandemic, there are many less bizarre or dramatic ways for a virus to move from animal to human.

Ignoring all of the information in science and teachings of history and preying on people's fear in order to propagate conspiracy theories and racist rhetoric is very damaging. And of course, when fear and misinformation are reinforced by the upper levels of leadership in a community or a county, two very dangerous things (among myriad negative effects) tend to happen:

One thing this rhetoric from the top leads to is "othering" the targeted group. "Othering" makes individuals in a group feel hurt, targeted, victimized, hopeless, and more vulnerable than the rest of the population because they are being singled out and harassed based on characteristics they cannot change. When a single group experiences significantly more chronic anxiety, repercussions can last long after the virus is under control. The effect of that anxiety can ripple throughout our social fabric for years afterwards.

The second thing is that by focusing on the virus having roots in places outside of the U.S., people who aren't from that place might not think that they are susceptible to the virus, and therefore might not take the precautions necessary to prevent further spread. That puts everybody's health at risk (in the case of this latest pandemic, not wearing masks, not washing hands, not social distancing), and may lead to other unintended consequences mired in discrimination. For example, the 2009–2010 H1N1 flu first recorded in the U.S. was *not* called the "American flu" but rather the "swine flu." Meanwhile, there were suggestions in the media that the flu came from Mexico, which then played into fears about immigration from our Southern border.

act ⎯⎯⎯⎯⎯⎯⎯⎯⎯⎯⎯⎯⎯⎯⎯⎯⎯⎯⎯

What should I do when I hear people being so hateful about COVID-19?

It's important to dispel myths about terms like the "China flu." If someone calls it that in front of or within earshot of you—or the "China virus" or "kung flu—interrupt them with a correction. You can gently say, "Oh, you mean COVID-19?" or, if you are feeling bold you can say, "I find that term offensive and incorrect." You've seen the statistics now; there has been a measured increase in discrimination and hate against people of Asian descent ever since the virus arrived on our shores. At various stages of the pandemic, Misasha and Sara both worried about their Japanese parents going out to do food shopping, in the off chance that they'd came across someone who was so ignited by the racist rhetoric that they'd hurt our parents. It's called a coronavirus simply based on the fact that the shape of the virus's surface looks sort of like a crown, and it's important not to play into the stigma of blaming Asian people for a virus that is entirely out of their control.

If in an encounter there seems to be an opportunity to have a safe and productive discussion, please go on to explain to the person who used the insensitive term why stereotyping groups of people is harmful.

This won't be the last virus that we will see. Stand up against policies that seem to not make logical sense, like only banning Chinese nationals from entering the United States rather than limiting all people who are entering from nations known to have high rates of illness. This country has a long history of looking down on immigrants, treating them in ways that we would not consider treating White Americans. From quarantine methods that centered only on immigrants, to naming viruses and diseases based on locations outside of our country while not owning up to diseases that start within our borders, to, most recently, hateful rhetoric being used and repeated by the top leaders in our nation and thus emboldening individuals to target all sorts of Asian people with vitriol, hateful words, and even violence. We are a country that has historically "othered" people who we want to cast aside. However, the entire population of our country—aside from Native Americans—has been built on immigration. **It's time we realize how harmful words—including virus names—can be, and the repercussions they have in the everyday lives of Americans.**

CHAPTER 18

Fancy Asians vs. Jungle Asians

listen

When her children were small, Sara spoke with them in Japanese. One day while out for a walk, a young White neighbor asked his mom why Sara was talking to them like that. When the mom explained that Sara was Japanese, the small boy replied with a knowing look, and said "Ohhh yeah, I can see some of that," as he tugged at the corner of his eyes to make them a little smaller and slantier.

To some White people, all Asians look the same, based on generalizations about hair texture and color, eye shape, skin tone.

But in her poignant stand-up show *Baby Cobra*, renowned comedian Ali Wong calls out racism between Asian ethnicities in a skit about "fancy Asians vs. jungle Asians."

She says, "You guys know the difference—the fancy Asians are the Chinese, the Japanese, they get to do fancy things like host the Olympics. Jungle Asians host diseases. It's . . . different." Based on the laughter you hear in the audience, people get it. She hits upon a truth that is uncomfortable yet widely understood.

Simply put, not all Asians are the same. There are distinct cultures and languages and yes, even racism, between the countries that are often lumped into the grouping of "Asian." In the case of the comedy skit, "Fancy Asian" refers to those from East Asia, which is generally understood as China, Korea, and Japan. "Jungle Asian" tends to mean Southeast Asia, which encompasses Vietnam, Thailand, the Philippines, Indonesia, Malaysia, Singapore, Cambodia, Laos, and Myanmar.

When people look at the vast multiplicity of Asian nations and descent and people as a single homogenous group, it erases the different identities and histories and tensions—good and bad—between many countries and cultures. It also diminishes the personal struggles for identity that Asian people go through in the United States. That's a problem.

learn—

The Model Minority

One of the most harmful stereotypes of Asian Americans is that of the "model minority." The model minority demographic has members who are seen to have achieved higher socioeconomic status than the average population, and so shouldn't need any governmental support. This myth stereotypes all Asian Americans as part of a monolithic group that works hard, is polite, law-abiding, and generally humble and successful.

The term "model minority" was coined by a sociologist named William Petersen in 1966, when he wrote a piece holding up the success of Japanese Americans and their ability to overcome discrimination, saying it is due to their family structure and culture of hard work. As part of the stereotype, Asian students are seen as being good at math; their mothers, now referred to as "tiger moms," enforce strict piano or violin practices and expect nothing but A+ on report cards; their fathers tend to be slight-framed, nerdy but successful people involved in some sort of scientific or numbers-oriented career. As stereotypes go, it seems like a great thing to be called, right? Nope.

What Petersen's paper did not take into account was that just one year earlier, the Immigration and Naturalization Act (aka Hart-Celler Act) had gotten rid of previous immigration restrictions that were basically a quota system based on what country you were from—until that point, there was very, very, very limited immigration allowed from Asia—and replaced them with a policy that put emphasis on categories like family reunification, skilled labor, and refugees. That meant that after allowing in families of people who were already in the United States, the next tier of immigrants admitted were professionals and scientists. What was the upshot? After 1965, a whole bunch of doctors and engineers from Asia immigrated to the United States.

> **MICROAGGRESSION:** Asking an Asian person for help with a math problem

It wasn't so much that their inherent Asian-ness was a model, but that the first generation of immigrants allowed into the United States from Asia at that time consisted of people who had "successful" qualifications. The gates had finally opened to Asian immigrants, but they were selective gates. By referring to the model minority's perceived collective success without putting their arrival into historical context, people were able to point to Asian people and say, "See, they were able to overcome racism, *they* were able to make it." That attitude minimized then and still does now the struggles that other minorities, like Black people, have to face based on *their* history in this country. On an individual level, it also allows others to assume that Asians who don't attain expected levels of "success" must have some kind of deficiency or didn't make enough effort, for which they can be overlooked or made to feel inadequate. The model minority myth focuses on exceptionalism, and reduces the real-life identity struggles, discrimination, and harm Asian individuals experience.

Let's take a look at the history that led to these "model" immigrants arriving in the late twentieth century. The shocking limitations placed on Asian immigrants throughout our history may clarify the difference between what people see as parental motivation to drive their children to success, like a tiger mom, and the long-lasting effects of governmental policies on the racial composition of our country.

But First, Exclusion

Historically speaking, in its founding days, the United States didn't put restrictions on who was allowed into the country. Everybody was allowed in. The distinction between "types" of people came through policies like the Naturalization Act of 1790, which stated that only free White people of "good character" who had lived in the United States for two years or longer were allowed to apply for citizenship. Anybody could come in; only a select few White people could have the privileges of citizenship.

In the 1800s, after the War of 1812 between the United States and Great Britain—which, incidentally, was the last time the United States was invaded (and the last time the Capitol building was raided until January 6, 2021), and was also the war during which Francis Scott Key was so inspired by a flag being raised over Fort McHenry that he wrote his poem "The Star-Spangled Banner"—there was a HUGE influx of White immigrants from Europe. Millions of Irish and German immigrants arrived over the course of several decades, in numbers large enough that it shifted the demographics of the country. As in, there were lots more White people who would eventually be allowed to become naturalized citizens.

After the Civil War, and after the abolition of slavery, there was a legal shunning of Asian people. The Naturalization Act of 1870 was passed, allowing citizenship to people of European and African descent. Black people were now finally allowed citizenship, but the policy excluded the thousands of Asian workers already in the United States, many of whom had provided labor during the Gold Rush and built the transcontinental railroad.

Enter another phase of immigration. Between 1880 and 1920, when the United States was experiencing urbanization and industrialization, immigrants arrived mainly from Central, Eastern, and Southern Europe. Many millions of White people entered the country; why weren't there more Asian immigrants?

For one, the Chinese Exclusion Act of 1882, which we talk about in Chapter 17, was enacted (see page 173). It was the first American policy that restricted one particular ethnic group from immigration. Until this point, there had been about thirty years of a small but steady influx of Chinese immigrants, and while they only made up 0.002 percent of the United States population (compared to the millions of Irish and German immigrants thus far), White workers blamed the Chinese for low wages. The Exclusion Act suspended the immigration of both skilled and unskilled Chinese laborers for ten years; Congress agreed to extend that suspension for another ten years in the Geary Act of 1892.

Then, around 1900, due to the strengthening war power of Japan within Asia, people started seeing Japanese people as threats, leading to the "Yellow Peril" stereotype. The stereotype encompassed all Asians, painting them as sneaky, dangerous foreigners who couldn't be trusted.

Although there had been a policy from 1894 that allowed open immigration between Japan and the United States, as an increased number of Japanese immigrants arrived in California, they were met with more resistance from locals. By the time the San Francisco Board of Education passed a regulation in 1906 requiring children of Japanese descent to attend separate schools, Japanese immigrants made up about 1 percent of California's population. In reaction to school segregation and other offensive policies, Japan and the United States signed the Gentleman's Agreement in 1907 that said Japan would purposely limit immigration to the U.S., allowing only professionals and businessmen to come over, if the separate-but-equal schooling policy were to be reversed. So not only were Chinese immigrants excluded, but Japanese immigrants were severely curtailed as well.

In the Immigration Act of 1917, legislation outlined an "Asiatic Barred Zone"—specific areas from which people could not immigrate, which included nearly all of Asia aside from Japan and the Philippines; it offered only several occupation-based exemptions. And after World War I, in a particularly restrictive move, President Calvin Coolidge signed the Immigration Act of 1924, which set a quota that only 2 percent of the total number of people in the United States of a certain country's nationality as of the 1890 census could obtain visas. Recall that many White immigrants had already come over from Europe prior to World War I, and so this percentage-based policy allowed relatively more Europeans to enter. In contrast, given policies like the Naturalization Act of 1870 and the Chinese Exclusion Act of 1882, which had kept Asian immigration and naturalization at relatively low numbers, this immigration act severely limited any Asians from migrating to the United States.

As a final nail in the coffin, the United States began limiting immigration from the Philippines. The Philippines was a colony of the United States at the time, and as such, Filipinos had been allowed to come to the mainland any time they wanted. But along with this wave of anti-Asian sentiment, Congress passed the Tydings-McDuffie Act in 1934, which said they'd give independence to the Philippines in 1945. In so doing, the United States could impose a limit of only fifty individual Filipino immigrants per year. Voilà: No more Asian influx.

As a result of legal immigration policy instigated and perpetuated by "othering" people of Asian descent, they comprised a relatively small population of people in the United States by the time World War II started. That set the stage for an absolutely horrific, inhumane decision by the government.

Japanese internment.

After the bombing of Pearl Harbor during World War II, Executive Order 9066 set up internment camps to house the Japanese Americans who lived within one hundred miles of the West Coast. They swept up nearly 120,000 people, two-thirds of whom were estimated to have been born in the United States and full citizens of this country. (While naturalization was still limited, a Supreme Court Case in 1898, *US v Wong Kim Ark*, established the idea of birthright citizenship: Regardless of racial or national origin, if you were born in the United States, you were a United States citizen.) In a HUGE civil rights violation, the government ripped many thousands of American citizens of Japanese ancestry out of their homes, took possession of their property, and held them hostage for the duration of the war, justifying it as a "military necessity." In a summary from the Immigration History blog, we see the stark contrast between the treatment of Japanese Americans and the fact that "Italian and German Americans suspected of conspiring with enemies of the United States were handled as individuals based on specific evidence of acting as 'enemy aliens.'"

While it's hard, it may make a penetrating point: Imagine a war between your kids' and a neighboring school. A brunette from the other school did something to hurt your kids' school, so your school herded up all of the brunettes in their own school and locked them away in barren conditions for years until the war was over, just in case they had allegiance with the brunette from the enemy school, because they look alike. Oh, and the brunettes would never get their belongings back from their lockers, because it was all taken over by the blondes. I mean it sounds ludicrous, but it shows just how far the United States took this unconstitutional and horrific roundup. Japanese had been seen as less than equal, and that, combined with the relative ease of differentiating people's Japanese features from White features versus differentiating Italian and German Whites, led to Japanese people being harshly punished for being born with Asian features.

All of this was less than a century ago. As we mentioned at the beginning of this section, it was only in 1965 that immigration policies shifted and no longer used race as a barrier, but instead became a category-based system. When more doors opened, there was a huge influx of immigrants escaping violence in Vietnam and Cambodia. Whereas in the 1950s more than half of all immigrants were Europeans and only 6 percent were Asians, by the 1990s only 16 percent were Europeans and 31 percent were of Asian descent.

As the Japanese American Citizens League (JACL) notes, "Since 1970 when the Census Bureau counted approximately 1.5 million Asian Americans, or less than one percent of the total United States population, the growth in the Asian American population has been dramatic. By 2000, there were nearly 12 million Asian Americans, comprising 4.2 percent of the population." We have seen more Asians entering our country during our lifetimes than in the nearly one hundred years prior.

The United States has a sordid history of discrimination against those from Asia; even today, despite the increased population of people from various countries within Asia and the many American-born citizens of Asian descent, the U.S. government still tends to lump all Asians together in the official statistics. While it can be useful to categorize groups of people from world regions for the purposes of harnessing the collective power of people of Asian origin (now often referred to as Asian American and Pacific Islander, or AAPI), lumping all Asians under one umbrella does a lot of harm. How?

First, it obviously ignores and annuls the diversity found in the many Asian countries. There are people of Chinese, Korean, Japanese, Vietnamese, Cambodian, Filipino, Indonesian, Thai, Indian, Singaporean, Malaysian, and Nepalese descent (and dozens more), and each one of these countries has a different culture that should be honored. Like people of all races and ethnicities, every Asian person is an individual with a different story.

Ignoring diversity also allows us to ignore the huge disparities that are seen in things like pay within the Asian community. For example, for every dollar that a Chinese American woman makes, a Cambodian American woman makes $0.57. It also then leads us to ignore very visible representations of difference within Asian careers: on the East Coast, for example, Korean nail salons catering to White women are common, whereas on the West Coast, Vietnamese-run nail salons are the norm. Yet, even within those differences, we can't remember the last time we went to a nail salon where a White woman painted shellac onto our hands and feet.

Furthermore, this generalizing prevents Asians from being seen as Americans; generations later, we continue to see them as foreigners. As long as the media portrays Asians as caricatures of themselves, the kung-fu fighting man or meek permissive woman, these stereotypes will persist. It means Misasha and Sara will continue to be asked, "Where are you from?" and the answer "California" or "Colorado" will not be good enough. We have to dig into our heritage and explain that one of our parents is from Japan. If you identify as White, consider whether you have been asked repeatedly where you are from, and if so, even after answering, do you then have to explain your European heritage in detail?

> **MICROAGGRESSION: Pressing an Asian person to tell you where they're *really* from**

Ultimately, this attitude lets people discount the possibility of racism against Asian people. While COVID-19 brought race-based discrimination to the forefront, we aren't often taught just how inhospitable the United States has been to immigrants of Asian descent. We also aren't made aware that the fight against illegal immigration affects Asians. According to statistics from 2017, one out of every six illegal immigrants into the United States is from Asia, and each one of those people faces fears of deportation. Despite being held up as a model of citizenry, Asian immigrants do not always feel safe here.

The fight for equality and destigmatizing of Asian people is a relatively new development in the United States; the population has only recently been allowed to grow. The monolith of "Asian" consists of a diverse array of people ranging from those whose ancestors were allowed to emigrate based on their professional or business acumen to descendants of laborers to those who have only recently left their countries to set up shop and make a better life for themselves and their families in this country.

It's important to note that the Asian struggle stands in contrast to the fight for equity and destigmatizing of Black people who were enslaved in this country for hundreds of years. Most Black Americans do NOT know their ancestors' country of origin because slavery ripped them out of their homes centuries ago; they've since been labeled based on the color of their skin. There are also more recent Black immigrants from Africa and the Caribbean, or children of immigrants, who proudly honor the traditions of their forefathers' countries. By suggesting that Asians are "models of success" implies that, similarly, Black people should be able to help themselves in their struggle for equality just by better applying themselves. Comparing groups without acknowledging their different immigration histories erases the entire struggle of racism that all minorities face in the United States.

act

What do I call Asians? Do I have to know their ancestors' country of origin?

Generally speaking, it's okay to refer to people as Asian—so long as their ethnic identity is relevant to a story or situation. In terms of this chapter, though, the main takeaway is to recognize that stereotypes are dehumanizing. We need to avoid phrases like "model minority," which separates Asians in general from other people of color and specifically removes them from the civil rights struggles of Black Americans—even though they are also still very much an underrepresented part of our country. Depending on the circumstance, splitting and lumping together racial identities both serve to create a wedge between Asians and others—in particular Black people—who continue to all fight against racism (see Chapter 12, page 112). We also want to avoid and interrupt people who use harmful slurs like Oriental or yellow, or worse. Even writing those words makes us cringe. Do not allow those insults to go unchecked.

Take notice when the appearance of an Asian person, the stereotypically smaller eyes or the silkier black hair, leads you to assume that they are an immigrant, or that they speak a different language than you—and consider that they are probably just as American as you are. We tend not to be as good at differentiating between people who don't look like us, so pay extra attention to specific characteristics of the people you meet so you don't mistake them for someone else. Learn how to pronounce people's names. Listen to their stories. **Question what you actually know about the person who is being stereotyped as the Tiger Mom or the math whiz, and get to know individuals and their family stories before assuming they're doing something because that's just their heritage.** If they tell you they're American, leave it at that and don't ask them to tell you all about where they're "really" from.

How do I get my kids (and my friends!) beyond thinking all Asians are the same nationality?

Can you tell we like books? Look again at the books you have in your child's home library, and bring in books featuring Asian characters that don't perpetuate stereotypes or only place Asian people within their ancient cultures. Expose them to stories featuring Asian people doing typically American things. Check out our list of favorite books in this realm (see Recommendations, page 225). Consider reading books authored by Asian Americans, beautiful novels like *Everything I Never Told You* by Celeste Ng, as well as history books like Ellen D Wu's *The Color of Success*.

Lastly, become familiar with the names and work of activists who have fought for Asian American rights, like Grace Lee Boggs or Yuri Kochiyama. For your kids, consider adding books like *Rad American Women A to Z* that feature powerful women from all across the spectrum.

CHAPTER 19

Who Is Latinx, Anyway?

According to the Pew Research Center, in 2017 there were nearly 60 million Latinos in the United States, accounting for approximately 18 percent of the total U.S. population.

Immigrants are a declining proportion of this group, making up 33 percent of the total number—down from 37 percent in 2010 due to slowing migration from Latin America. (If you've got questions about immigration, we've devoted all of Chapter 21 to that issue.). **In fact, 79 percent of Latinos living in the United States are citizens.** They are often long-time U.S. residents, speak English proficiently, and live in metropolitan areas (though the communities vary distinctly by country of origin depending on which area of the country they live in).

Latino American income levels differ between nationalities, sometimes significantly. In 2018, Argentines had the highest median household income at $68,000, almost $20,000 more than the overall Latino median ($49,010); Hondurans had the lowest median income at $41,000, about $8,000 lower than the Latino median; and Mexicans had a median income ($49,000) similar to the overall Latino median. For reference, the median American household income in 2018 was $63,179.

So there are some facts about Latinos as a group, and some that point to significant differences between people grouped under that term. If you're reading this and you're like us, you're probably asking yourself a key question: What's the difference between terms like Latino, Latina, and Latinx? What about Hispanic, and Chicano? Which countries make up which groups, and why do all these terms and distinctions matter anyway?

listen

As we were writing this chapter, Joe Biden, then president-elect of the United States, announced a historic nomination: the first Latino ever to serve as the head of the Department of Homeland Security. And, perhaps even more fittingly, his nominee, Alejandro Mayorkas, is not only the first Latino, but the first immigrant in this role of overseeing American immigration policies and procedures—a point we can't help but cheer about, as daughters of immigrants.

Mayorkas's immigrant story is similar to the stories of many refugees from Central America that we've heard. He is a refugee whose parents, seeking to escape from Castro's Cuba, came here when Alejandro was an infant. Along with so many others who fled in the night by way of boat or on foot or however they could, they came with hopes for a better life in the United States for themselves and their families.

Mayorkas's life in the U.S. is indeed an example of those kind of hopes realized. After his family fled Cuba in 1960, Alejandro grew up in Beverly Hills, graduated from Loyola Law School, and became an assistant U.S. attorney in the 1990s, prosecuting big names like "Hollywood Madam" Heidi Fleiss for money laundering. He later became the U.S. attorney for the Central District of California, where he oversaw the federal government's prosecution of drug cartels and White supremacists, and created a new office called the Civil Rights Section, which was focused on police misconduct and hate crimes.

But while Mayorkas's original immigration story may be similar to that of many refugees that we imagine from Central and South America, the subsequent trajectory is very different than the stories that we hear on the news regarding recent immigration. When we refer to Latinos, Latinas, or the Latinx population in the United States, we often believe—or let our words indicate—that this is a monolithic population, even though it represents a vast multiplicity of people, from Cuban immigrants who have been here for decades to Mexican Americans who have been here even longer to new immigrants from oppressive regimes in the Americas (Nicaragua and Venezuela, just to name a few—but the list is long if we widen the time frame). As the Pew Research Center further notes:

> Within this group [of immigrants], there are a number of countries and cultures represented. From 2010 to 2017, the Venezuelan population in the U.S. increased 76 percent to 421,000 in 2017, by far the fastest growth rate among Hispanic origin groups. Among groups with populations above 1 million, Dominicans and Guatemalans had the fastest growth. Their populations grew by 37 percent and 30 percent, respectively, during this time. Puerto Ricans, the second-largest origin group, saw their population in the 50 states and the District of Columbia jump by 20 percent, to 5.6 million in 2017. (Another 3.2 million live in Puerto Rico.) At nearly 37 million, Mexicans are the largest origin group and make up 62 percent of Latinos, but this share has decreased from a recent peak of 66 percent in 2008.

So once again, we have different groups coming to the U.S. at different times, with different beliefs. They can't be seen as a single unified group. We witnessed this borne out in the 2020 election, when Latinx voters were in many ways treated as one bloc—but made very different decisions as to which candidate they ended up supporting.

That's why words like Latino/a, Hispanic, and Chicano matter so much.

If you aren't sure what the difference is between the three words above or what they even mean, we can relate. As history .com points out, "[t]he terms Latino, Hispanic and Latinx are often used interchangeably to describe a group that makes up about 18 percent of the U.S. population. While it's now common to use umbrella terms to categorize those with ties to more than 20 Latin American countries, these words haven't always fostered a sense of community among the people they're supposed to describe."

Knowing the history behind each word and the differences inherent in them helps explain why the history of Latinx people in the United States is not a homogeneous one, and why we can't consider the Latinx population without understanding, and appreciating, the inherent nuances throughout its various communities.

learn

First, a quick definition of Latin America, so that we can orient ourselves geographically. According to *Britannica*, Latin America is "generally understood to consist of the entire continent of South America, in addition to Mexico, Central America, and the islands of the Caribbean whose inhabitants speak a Romance language (e.g. the Dominican Republic, Haiti, etc.). As you can tell, this is an extremely broad geographic area, but at least it provides some context. Now, let's narrow our scope a little.

If the larger geographic area is Latin America, who is "Hispanic"? Prior to the first usage of this designation on the federal census in 1980, anyone who came from Latin America was considered Spanish-speaking, but could either be "of Spanish origin" or "White" on the census. (That's why, even to this day, the U.S. Census data still differentiates "non-Hispanic White" in the data it collects. Have you ever considered Hispanic people to be White?) Census data is often used for resource allocation, which was problematic for many communities, including those of Mexican Americans, where activists complained that if they were considered White, they had "no data to prove that their communities needed resources for programs, such as job training."

In order for these communities to get resources, two very separate groups, Puerto Ricans and Mexicans, needed to be aligned and allied to petition together for having their ethnicity reflected on the census. The uniting of these two very different groups is central to the development of not only the term "Hispanic" but the concept of a singular "Latino" narrative. The Puerto Rican and Mexican immigration stories were different from the start, both in terms of their paths to immigration and the physical locations of their communities once in the United States. They're culturally and politically different, and in turn faced significant differences in treatment by the federal government. There was no natural alliance between these two groups. In order to understand this point, we have to look first at their different immigration stories.

Mexico

Two distinct events caused Mexican migration to the United States. First, at the end of the Mexican-American War in 1848, the Republic of Mexico gave the United States more than one-third of its former territory, which included the current states of California, Nevada, Utah, Arizona, New Mexico, Colorado, Texas, and parts of Oklahoma, Kansas, and Wyoming. From the American side, the peace treaty "offered blanket naturalization to the estimated 75,000 to 100,000 former citizens of Mexico who chose to remain in these new American territories at the end of the war." Around the same time, an additional 10,000 Mexican miners came to California during the Gold Rush.

The second wave of migration started close to the 1900s, when U.S. employers, needing another labor source due to rapid economic development (and the restrictive, discriminatory laws against Asian immigration), looked south for workers needed in industries like agriculture, mining, construction, and transportation (in particular, with regard to the burgeoning railroad development and maintenance). More than 100,000 Mexicans migrated to the United States during this period, and the Mexican War kept immigration strong from 1910 until around 1930. At this time, the total Mexican or Mexican American population of the United States was at least 1.5 million, with the majority in Texas, California, and Arizona, and another significant group working in industrial jobs in the Midwest, especially in major cities like Chicago, Detroit, and Gary, Indiana.

MICROAGGRESSION: Assuming people who look Hispanic don't speak English well

Despite benefiting from their labor until this point, the U.S. conducted a mass "repatriation" of Mexicans and Mexican Americans. From 1929–1936, an unspecified number of Mexicans and Mexican Americans (estimates range from 350,000 to 1 million) were forced to leave the United States for Mexico, a country that for many wasn't theirs from the start (as with those Mexican Americans who were citizens of the United States by birth, and identified as American). The Mexican government was wary of the changing immigration patterns imposed on it by the U.S. over the years (aka deporting Mexicans and U.S. citizens alike back to Mexico), but despite this, in 1942, the U.S. and Mexico signed the Mexican Farm Labor Agreement, as the United States was facing yet another labor shortage in World War II.

By reopening the southern border between the United States and Mexico, the agreement, also called the "Bracero" program (from the Spanish word for manual labor), created not only a rise in authorized immigration, but a rise in undocumented immigration as well; for decades, the program was seen as offering better opportunities to many who were struggling in Mexico. The official program lasted twenty-four years, a period over which American employers helped support not only the documented migration but also the undocumented migration—with the latter, they benefited from cheap labor while avoiding the red tape and higher costs associated with having to deal with the program. It is thought by some that the Bracero program changed both American economic practices and demographics on a scale that few could have imagined at its outset.

Puerto Rico

Puerto Rico has a completely different history with the U.S. When Spain lost the Spanish-American War of 1898, the island of Puerto Rico became an "unincorporated territory" of the United States. The Foraker Act of 1900 gave the United States the ability to create a civil government on Puerto Rico, including a governor that was appointed by the president of the United States, a mixed American and Puerto Rican executive council (where the Americans outnumbered the Puerto Ricans by one, ensuring an American majority), and an American court system. Not surprisingly, that didn't go over so well with Puerto Rico.

In 1917, Congress passed the Jones Act, which provided Puerto Rico with some provisions for independent governance, including a bicameral legislature (with American oversight still in place) and a Puerto Rican Bill of Rights. It also granted U.S. citizenship to all Puerto Ricans, unless they chose to renounce this offer—of which three hundred Puerto Ricans did, choosing to remain independent instead.

Instead of levying control over Puerto Rico as a colony, the very act of conferring citizenship on Puerto Ricans gave them the right to migrate anywhere within the jurisdiction of the United States, and gave them full rights as citizens—minus the right to vote. One of the unintended consequences of the Jones Act was to encourage these new American citizens to leave Puerto Rico and utilize their new status to live in the continental United States. As the island's main income source, sugar production, began to wane, many Puerto Ricans moved to the continent, and in particular to New York City. Once in New York, many became low-wage workers in the garment industry, but a significant number also became entrepreneurs, filling specific needs for Puerto Rican cultural goods and services as the area's population continued to grow. World War II, and a failed American government–sponsored plan to help Puerto Rico after the war, led to even more migration from Puerto Rico to the continental United States. By 1960, close to 900,000 Puerto Ricans were living on the mainland.

Uniting Two Distinct Groups

So, from these short descriptions we can see how Mexico and Puerto Rico are not only geographically distinct, but also politically, socially, economically, and culturally distinct. Trying to fit these two groups comfortably and viably under the umbrella of a single descriptive term posed a monumental feat, to say the least. "Hispanic" became the term that many groups, including politicians and the census bureau, thought would work because it was linked to the Spanish word *hispano* (referring to natives or descendants of Spanish settlers in the Southwest before it was annexed to the United States) but seemed more "American." For census purposes, "Hispanic" refers to those from Spain and other Spanish-speaking countries, which therefore excludes Brazilians, as Portuguese, not Spanish, is the official language of Brazil.

Back to our census story. While "Hispanic" was introduced in the 1980 census, it didn't really gain traction until the 1990s, when two rounds of censuses, along with new directions and presence in the media—especially through entities that catered to the Spanish-speaking population like Univision and Telemundo—helped to unite these distinct communities under one appellation.

While for a time our society had a term that served to unify a group of different communities, largely for the purposes of resource allocation but also growingly in people's needs for social and popular culture reference points, a collective seeking for other terms persisted and evolved. The term "Hispanic," which seemed to be Spain-centered, got some pushback because Spain had colonized much of Latin America, and many felt that wasn't a characteristic to highlight or celebrate. The term "Latino," which referred to people from Latin America (thereby including Brazil but not Spain) and had started to appear in popular culture in the 1970s, resurfaced as an alternative in the late 1990s. According to Ramón A. Gutiérrez, a Preston and Sterling Morton Distinguished Service Professor of United States history at the University of Chicago, Latino "was previously a Spanish-language word that came from *Latino America*, which Colombian writer José María Torres Caicedo helped popularize." It is short for *Latino Americano*, and the abbreviated words *hispano* and *latino* were in use among Spanish speakers in California from the mid-1800s. But by the 1920s, other terms had replaced them—until writers and pop culture brought them back because the nuances between the terms were becoming increasingly important.

"Latino" first appeared on the census in 2000, included in the question "Is this person Spanish/Hispanic/Latino?" While this new term deemphasized the Spanish connection, it wasn't enough for some individuals, who picked their origin nationalities over being labeled Spanish, Hispanic, or Latino. Notably, according to a Pew Research Center 2013 study, only 20 percent of respondents described themselves as Hispanic or Latino. Meanwhile, 54 percent used "their family's Hispanic origin term (such as Mexican, Cuban, Salvadoran) to identify themselves" and 23 percent used "American."

The word "Chicano" came to resonate with some Mexicans who didn't feel connected with either Latino or Hispanic. It's unclear where the word came from, but there are several theories, including that "it comes from *mexicano* (pronounced meshicano), a word that some 'groups of Nahuas (Indigenous speakers of Nahuatl) began calling their language,'" writes David Bowles, an author and professor at the University of Texas Rio Grande Valley. Chicano may be a nickname form of "Mexicano," or a shortened form that drops the first syllable of the full term, that just stuck.

On the other hand, Chicano may first have been used as a slur, as one of the first mentions in print is in the Texas-based Spanish-language newspaper *La Crónica* in 1911, where the word was used to describe "less cultured" Mexican Americans and recent immigrants. By the 1960s, the name was taken up proudly among Mexican American activists fighting for civil rights—to whatever degree "Chicano" had been used as a slur, this would seem to be a reclaiming of an offensive word to take back power. (For a discussion of this in the Black context, page 101, "Isn't the N-Word Okay Sometimes?")

With three terms, Hispanic, Latino, and Chicano, in active use for these diverse immigrant populations, some individuals still prefer to identify as either just American, or by their specific nationality. And in a recent evolution of the nomenclature, because Spanish is a gendered language, with "Latino" and "Latina" embedded with gender specificity, in order to include gender non-binary individuals, the term Latinx was created.

While the creation of, need for, and even pronunciation of Latinx is being debated, it's unclear when, how, or who put the word into circulation, although it appears to have been first used in the early 2000s. In August 2020, the Pew Research Center found that only 3 percent of Latinos use Latinx, but it is a term that has gained popular and social momentum since inception, as it's been adopted in both print and other forms of media.

act

What do we do with the knowledge that we have now of the differences, and difficulties, in trying to call such diverse groups of people, with perhaps more differences than commonalities, by one label?

Perhaps the biggest takeaway is that people should be able to define their own identities. If you're not sure how someone identifies, rather than making assumptions about who identifies as Latino/Latina/Latinx, Hispanic, or Chicano/Chicana, ask. **Asking is always better than assuming, and we should constantly be reinforcing that with our kids through modeling and conversation.** If you are talking to or about a specific person, it's helpful to know their exact country of origin to be able to reference that if needed, as opposed to relying on sometimes overbroad, sometimes incorrect terminology.

These different communities also tend to support specific policies and political candidates for reasons that make sense to their individual experiences, not their experiences as one Hispanic or Latino monolith in the United States. **Respect these differences and highlight and support that they exist in all possible forums, rather than take them for granted.** Getting involved with different community-based organizations that focus on the different groups that are most prevalent in your communities, especially ones where you and your kids can learn together, is a great way to start. You can also look for groups that support the causes you believe in, such as immigrant rights and education (the Hispanic Scholarship Fund and the Committee for Hispanic Children and Families are two that we like). Or, because we live in a bilingual society, follow the lead of your kids' at school and learn some Spanish. (Your kids may love teaching you something as well!) Also, if someone is speaking English with an accent, that means they are at least bilingual if not multilingual. That's something to be celebrated, period. It's never okay to make fun of someone's accented English.

MICROAGGRESSION: Imitating a person's accent

Last but not least, never forget the power of voting with your wallet. Choose to shop at stores that give back to the communities or brands whose founders are Latinx (Beautyblender—yes, THAT makeup sponge—Cuyana, and Kids of Immigrants are favorites around here). An easy Internet search will provide lists of businesses in your area, as well as those that you can support online.

We began this chapter with a question: Who is Latinx, anyway? Our best response to this is: "Whoever says they are."

CHAPTER 20

Native Americans: When an Entire Race Disappears from Modern History

Not so long ago, growing up in Pasadena meant that part of every elementary school kid's field trip repertoire included a trip to the now-defunct Southwest Museum, which was on a hill in the Arroyo Seco and was the brainchild of Charles Fletcher Lummis, an anthropologist, historian, journalist, and photographer. The museum opened in its Pasadena location in 1914, making it the oldest museum in town, and served as a home for what some called one of the "most important" collections of Native American art and artifacts.

While the museum no longer exists, Misasha remembers that field trip. Well, to be specific, she remembers walking into the room with the huge Native American teepee and being amazed at how impressive it was. If you had asked her at the time if all Native Americans lived in teepees, she probably would have said yes. Because that's what she had learned in history textbooks, and had seen in "real" (museum) life, with no other narrative to provide a counterpoint. In her nine-year-old mind, the Native Americans were frozen in time around 1900. Teepees and all.

listen ⎯⎯⎯⎯⎯⎯⎯⎯⎯⎯⎯⎯⎯⎯⎯

If the timeline of Native American history you were taught in school pretty much ended in 1900, you're not alone. On the podcast back in 2019, Crystal Echo Hawk opened our eyes in a huge way to the Native people and the ways that they have been shut out of the dominant American narrative. Crystal is an enrolled citizen of the Pawnee Nation of Oklahoma and president and CEO of IllumiNative. In 2018, IllumiNative released a groundbreaking study called Reclaiming Native Truth (RNT), the largest public opinion research and strategy-setting initiative ever conducted for and about Native Americans. Not surprisingly, RNT concluded that pop culture, media, and K–12 education continue to drive and perpetuate negative stereotypes and myths connected to Native culture, and has led to the erasure of Native peoples from our collective history.

Part of the RNT study looked at representation and portrayals of Natives in American culture. In particular, there are so many contradictory presentations of Natives (all created by non-Natives) that it's difficult to even fathom what the truths may actually be. As the study notes: "Faulty history lessons, media reports and rumors leave people with the false assumption that individual Native Americans are not U.S. citizens, receive money from the government, don't pay taxes, are rich from casinos, and/or go to college for free (all untrue). 'Positive' stereotypes blend many unique tribes into one 'Native American' persona that is perceived to be committed to family and culture, spiritual and mystical, resilient through historical challenges, fiercely protective of the land, and patriotic to the United States. Non-Natives often hold positive and negative stereotypes together: Native peoples living in poverty and rich from casinos; resilient and addicted to drugs and alcohol; the noble warrior and savage warrior." In particular, Crystal elucidated for us, we are taught about Native history through history created by non-Natives, and so that history often ends around the turn of the century—the last century. The RNT found that 87 percent of schools in the United States don't teach about Native peoples beyond 1900.

As a result, according to the RNT, 72 percent of Americans know little to nothing about Natives; and 72 percent of Americans rarely or *never* encounter information about Native People in this society. When you consider how we're constantly inundated with information, that's shocking. Crystal noted that in Oklahoma, which is her home state, "with our thirty-nine tribes in the state, we represent about 10 percent of the state population. We're one of the larger populations, statewide. And yet, we're only represented 0.8 percent within the Social Studies curriculum. So even here in the state, reservations are everywhere and most Oklahomans aren't learning about us."

One study found that when you type the words "Native American" into a search engine, 95 percent of the images that come up are pre-1900, and are almost always men. As a result, Native Americans are being erased from modern history—and the history that has been taught to us centers around contrasting views created by non-Natives. If that's the case, what is the very minimum we need to know about the history that we *aren't* being taught?

learn

The Wampanoag Tribe, also known as the People of the First Light, have inhabited the eastern coast of present-day Massachusetts for *more than twelve thousand years*. Let's just take that in for a second: In terms of a group of people living on Earth, twelve thousand years is not a time frame that we can easily fathom.

It is the Wampanoag Tribe who were the Native Americans present at the First Thanksgiving we teach our grade school children about, and largely forms the start of any K–12 education regarding Native Americans. However, as has been highlighted in recent years, that narrative has largely been whitewashed to remove the destruction of the Wampanoag that took place at the hands of the Pilgrims. As *Time* notes in a detailed article about what really happened when the *Mayflower* sailed to America, after docking the *Mayflower* in 1620, the Pilgrims left to find better land and ran into the Wampanoag tribe. They built Plymouth Colony on their land.

They also brought "plague and disease and pretty much almost wiped us out, so it's not so much a cause for celebration," says Kitty Hendricks-Miller, who is the Indian Education Coordinator at the Mashpee Wampanoag Tribe. As a result, Thanksgiving is not a celebration for the Wampanoag, but rather a day of mourning the epidemic and the centuries of Native American removal policies that followed—including the start of the erasure of Native Americans from our collective history.

Consider this story that was shared, also in *TIME*, from that same tribe:

> When Paula Peters was in second grade in Philadelphia in the
> mid-1960s, listening to a teacher talk about Plymouth Colony
> and the Mayflower, a student asked what happened to the Native
> Americans who helped the Pilgrims settle, the Wampanoag. The
> teacher said they were all dead. "When she mentioned we're all
> dead, that was devastating. . . . I raised my hand, and I said, no
> that's not true, I'm a Wampanoag, and I'm still here. I didn't
> know enough then as a second grader that I could challenge
> her, but I think that I've challenged that second-grade teacher
> ever since. Part of my everyday being is telling people that we're
> still here."

They're thought of as dead. Forgotten. Disappeared. After that fateful first Thanksgiving, timelines regarding Native American history are sparse, focusing on the forced removal of Native Americans and all of the federal government acts and military battles waged against the Native Americans, often resulting in huge casualties suffered by the Native peoples. (And trust us, we looked at a lot.) After the Native Americans were "safely" relocated to reservations, we didn't hear much about them—which seems to make sense, given how the dominant narrative largely regarded Native Americans as a threat because of land rights, until they were suddenly not anymore. And then, like all neutralized threats, they were marginalized right out of the narrative.

There's little left to concretely demonstrate the contributions that Native Americans have made to contemporary life—which is important, as RNT duly notes, because history "must be directly linked to contemporary life . . . Native Americans' cultures and contributions are vital parts of modern life." It's not enough to just point to Charles Curtis, who was the first Native American U.S. senator in 1907 and then became the first non-White vice president under Martin Van Buren—because Curtis spent much of his time in office grappling with his own forced assimilation into the dominant narrative. He was also inadvertently supporting policies that further led to Native assimilation, like segregated schools, due to his own lack of understanding as to the ramifications of his actions. It's not enough to know Jim Thorpe's name and his

Olympic gold medals; nor is it enough to know that Maria Tallchief was perhaps one of the most talented—yet discriminated against—ballerinas of her time.

Those are amazing individuals, yes, but knowing who they are is not enough to understand all Native Americans. In some ways it's amazing that these individuals were able to rise to the levels of success that they did considering the many ways that the United States government attempted to forcibly wipe out all memories of Native American life. Those segregated schools we just mentioned? They were actually part of the plan to effectively remove Native American culture and history—especially the inconvenient parts—from general American history.

"As [the White] population grew in the United States and people settled further west towards the Mississippi in the late 1800s, there was increasing pressure on the recently removed groups to give up some of their new land," according to the Minnesota Historical Society. Because they basically ran out of land to the west, the U.S. decided that the next best thing was to make Native Americans into White Americans. In 1885, Commissioner of Indian Affairs Hiram Price explained the logic: "[It] is cheaper to give them education than to fight them."

Enter schools like Carlisle School in Pennsylvania, which opened with the sole mission of assimilating Native American children. Carlisle was the first such school, and was the brainchild of a former U.S. cavalry officer, Captain Richard Henry Pratt, who felt that the only solution to the Native American "problem" was for Native Americans to assimilate. The way they got their students was simple: They coerced their parents to let them go, then took them from their homes and moved them to these boarding schools, thereby isolating these Native American children from their families and communities for years—or longer.

Notably, in 1892, Pratt said, "A great general has said that the only good Indian is a dead one, and that high sanction of his destruction has been an enormous factor in promoting Indian massacres. . . . In a sense, I agree with the sentiment, but only in this: that all the Indian there is in the race should be dead. Kill the Indian in him, and save the man." That last line effectively became the operating motto for Carlisle, which was run like a military academy, where Native American youth were under strict supervision, encountered corporal punishment, and were forced to learn trade skills separate from any Native American cultural ones.

Roughly one hundred and fifty boarding schools of this type were opened—and all were susceptible to deadly diseases like tuberculosis and the flu. Carlisle School was open for around thirty years (1879–1918), and in that time period close to two hundred children died and were buried on the school campus, thousands of miles away from their homes. Three of these children were from the Northern Arapahoe tribe, who were taken from their home in Wyoming on March 11, 1881, and sent to Carlisle, along with ten thousand other Native American children over the time period that the school was open.

Once there, these boys were given new names: Little Chief, fourteen, became Dickens Nor; Horse, eleven, became Horace Washington; and Little Plume, nine, was now Hayes Vanderbilt Friday. (If you're wondering who came up with these names, you're not alone—and records aren't clear as to how names were given.) They never got to use their Native names again, as all three boys died within two years of arriving at Carlisle and were buried in the small cemetery at school.

The Northern Arapahoe never forgot them, though. In 2016, the tribe petitioned the U.S. Army (currently, the Army War College is on the old school grounds) to release the remains. The government agreed, and also footed the $500,000 bill to exhume the three boys and ship their bodies back to their tribal burial grounds in Wyoming.

While that sounds like a small victory, and in truth does allow for some healing to begin, the relationship between White Americans and Native American burial grounds has been contentious at best. After the Civil War, the Surgeon General issued orders to Army medical personnel to collect Native American human remains for study. William Johnson, a Saginaw Chippewa citizen and curator at the Ziibiwing Center of Anishinabe Culture and Lifeways in Michigan, notes that "[i]t was believed that cranial capacity would provide insight into Native American personality and intelligence. . . . Native American graves were looted and craniums were collected in the name of science."

Ironically, the myth of the vanishing Native American led to further gravesite desecration at the turn of the century. Wealthy

White people, believing that Native people were relegated to history and not currently living in America, just in sovereign nations out of sight from White Americans, paid a lot of money to go on archeology expeditions because, as Johnson writes, they "believed that Native American people would be an extinct race, and therefore everything needed to be collected by any means necessary." The irony of both pushing a whole race into extinction and then using that extinction as a reason to collect anything left is not lost on us.

act ——————————————————

So what's next? How do we remember and highlight the work and lives of Native Americans when we have so much to learn?

First, it's important to learn terminology. As RNT notes:

- There are many diverse Native American peoples, cultures, and histories. We use the plural of each term intentionally.

- Different organizations use different terms to refer to the indigenous peoples of the Americas. Common terms are Native American, American Indian/Alaska Native (AI/AN), Native peoples, and Indigenous peoples. If you're from Canada, you may be familiar with the term First Nations as well.

- People are citizens, not members, of tribes. The preferred terms are tribal citizen, tribal nation, and Native nation. If you are talking about a specific Native nation and its citizens, use the tribe's name rather than the general term Native American. For example, say, "According to the tribal chairman of the Standing Rock Sioux Tribe" or "We spoke with Mary Smith, a citizen of the Navajo Nation." If you are unsure of how to refer to a tribal nation, check the tribe's website for the preferred terminology and full legal name.

Second, it is important to recognize that the history of Native Americans is one of great strength and revitalization, even in the face of pain, injustice, loss of land, removal and relocation, biased history, and derogatory sports mascots. It is built around respect for family and elders, responsibility to the land, and obligations to do right for and by future generations.

One great way to start is by researching the tribes who occupied the land where you live, where you work, where your kids go to school, if that is part of the history of the area where you live. The National Congress of American Indians has a great directory of tribal leaders that can give you more information or at least a place to start: https://ncai.org/tribal-directory. Certain areas of the country (California and Seattle come to mind) are making it possible for non-Native residents to pay a donation-based land tax to the tribes who originally occupied the same lands, thereby allowing tribes monetary means to reclaim their land as well as provide a form of symbolic reparations. That's something else you can check online to see if it's available in your area.

Equally important is to know what cultural appropriation is (the "sexy Pocahontas" costume that you might think is fun for Halloween but is someone else's cultural heritage), and what terms to avoid (for example, "powwow" is actually a Native American celebration that takes months to prepare, so you should avoid using that for a quick chat that has none of the same cultural meaning attached). And think about recent name changes of places and things—Squaw Valley to Olympic Valley, or the Washington Football Team—and let the appreciation sink in that offensive, appropriating names have been changed to ones that do not disrespect Native culture. Think about word—and clothing—choice before you use them. When in doubt, ask. Or do some research.

MICROAGGRESSION: Using offensive phrases like gypped, Indian giver, or "that's so gay"

Currently, there are more than six hundred sovereign Native nations, and Native Americans are in every profession and segment of society. If you don't know a Native American personally, here is your mandate: Go meet them. Find the tribes who are near you (as we discussed above), or somewhere that can share the history with you. RNT put together a publication called "Changing the Narrative: A Message Guide for Allies" in which you can find the organizations in your community, what groups they support, and how land rights are being addressed in your area of the country.

Together with your family, find ways in which you can change and question the narrative in your own spheres, including what your kids are being taught in school. Misasha's son recently started a Native American project in which kids in his class learned about a specific Native tribe in California. The primer which her son was given as part of this report creation uses outdated terms—it was written in 1992. One way to keep this conversation current in your kids' schools is to use (and recommend to teachers!) the resources listed above. If you remember Misasha's museum experience at the beginning of this chapter, when it comes to teaching about Native people and culture in our schools, not much has changed in at least a generation.

The RNT study ends on this positive wish: "[L]et's find our commonalities, celebrate our differences, and creatively work together for our shared future and the futures of the next generations." We couldn't agree more.

CHAPTER 21

Give Me Your Tired, Your Poor

As we wrote this book, and in particular, this chapter, we were coming out of a presidency that made immigration its primary focus. Over the course of the four years President Trump held office, there were more than four hundred policy changes aimed at narrowing both legal and illegal immigration options and ways into the United States. We heard about some of the biggest ones—the wall, children in cages, the Muslim Ban—but what was happening with regard to immigration was often much smaller, and more nefarious, than the stories covered in the press.

First: a word about what this chapter is not going to be about. There are so many negative and unwarranted stereotypes about immigrants out there that it would take a separate book to address all of these. Have you ever thought that immigrants make up a bigger portion of criminals than non-immigrants? That they're a drain on America because they come here illegally and are using resources that are meant for "true Americans"? That they're all Mexican? That they're stealing jobs meant for Americans? In spite of the rampant disinformation and conspiracy theories disseminated these last years, we've seen no stats that support any of these, and in fact, quite to the contrary. A 2016 Bureau of Prisons report shows that roughly 6 percent of inmates in state and federal prisons are not U.S. citizens. As of 2018, CNN reports that less than 4 percent of the total U.S. population is made up of undocumented immigrants; and only 13.7 percent of the total U.S. population is made up of immigrants (people born outside of the U.S.), a 2018 Pew Research report notes.

The same Pew Research study shows that while Mexico is the number one country for immigrants to the United States, it's not the only group by far. By region of birth, immigrants from Asia combined accounted for 28 percent of all immigrants in 2018, close but even larger than the share of immigrants from Mexico (25 percent). Other regions make up smaller shares: Europe, Canada, and other North America (13 percent); the Caribbean (10 percent); Central America (8 percent); South America (7 percent); the Middle East and North Africa (4 percent); and sub-Saharan Africa (5 percent).

In addition—those resources and jobs? In a study reported on by Forbes based on U.S. Census data from the past several censuses, immigrants were much more likely to create a business than native-born Americans. For example, where 0.83 percent of immigrants in the workforce started a business between 2005 and 2010, only 0.46 percent of native-born Americans did. Based on several factors, including the number of patents filed, the data also showed that businesses created by immigrants tended to be more innovative. In turn, this innovation translated into higher wages and higher-quality work product. In other words, they found that immigrants weren't necessarily taking jobs—they were creating them.

A word also about undocumented immigrants and jobs. *Scientific American* points out that they're doing the work that native-born Americans don't want to do. Undocumented immigrant workers are concentrated in agriculture (17 percent), construction (13 percent), and leisure and hospitality (9 percent). They also represent about 22 percent of the business and other services sector, which includes legal services, landscaping, waste management, and personal services (e.g., dry cleaners, manicurists, and car washers). By occupation, they hold a higher share of farming jobs (26 percent) when compared to their share of the workforce, and a lower share of maintenance, management, professional, sales, and office support jobs. A study from the Urban Institute revealed that, of 16 million workers in the United States without a high school diploma, immigrants and native-born workers actually do very different jobs, mostly due to experience and language issues. Minimum wage, menial jobs don't appeal to a lot of native-born

Americans. Those are the jobs that undocumented workers, or even legal immigrants without language skills or training, do—the jobs that we don't want to do ourselves, but that are necessary to keep our communities functioning.

All of this suggests that we should want more immigrants in this country. Except, for the past several years, we've done the exact opposite. For example, in 2019, the Trump administration created a rule that required all immigrants seeking asylum or other humanitarian relief to fill in *every space* on the application—even if the question didn't apply to them. If even one spot was left empty— for example, if they didn't fill out the middle name space because they don't have one—then that document would get rejected. That wasn't just a refiling hassle; it could derail their claims entirely, and possibly open the door to deportation. And this wasn't a one-time, one-form issue. It was "among hundreds of Trump administration changes in forms, regulations and fees that appear[ed] tiny and technical but that in combination significantly impact[ed] the nation's immigration system."

And more often than not, it impacted whole families—in particular, children.

listen

Have you heard of the Remain in Mexico Program? Under the Trump Administration, this program forced migrants seeking asylum in the United States to wait in Mexico while their claims were adjudicated—even if they weren't from Mexico in the first place. That means that Central Americans applying for asylum in the United States might be spending months, or even years, in Mexico waiting for an outcome of their application. That sounds ridiculously difficult to us as adults.

Now imagine that you're eleven. Or nine. Or seven.

According to *Time* magazine, young asylum-seekers in cities like Matamoros, Mexico, slept in tents that had been donated to them, and relied on food that volunteers from both sides of the border attempted to bring them on a daily basis. Volunteers said, "Asylum-seekers go to the restroom in portable bathrooms volunteers have rented using donated money while sanitary napkins, clothes, diapers, other supplies and medical care are also provided by donation." Shower tents allowed migrants the ability to use a bucket of water and a cup to bathe, but many also jumped in the Rio Grande to wash themselves and their clothes.

Volunteers also reported that children were, not surprisingly, traumatized by these forced living conditions, which sometimes resulted not only in family separation, but also presented larger, immediate threats to survival like rape, violence, and organized crime. Since the program began in January of 2019, some desperate asylum seekers tried, and failed, to swim their way to safety in the Rio Grande, drowning along the way.

Back to the most heartbreaking stories, the children. *Time* reported on pictures drawn by children held in these makeshift camps, in which their drawings "depict family members separated by the Rio Grande, children inside cages, and images of America. In one photo, a drawing by nine-year-old Genesis depicts crocodiles in a river near a vehicle she labelled '*Policía*.' Her family, in tears, stand in Mexico, while her *tía*, or aunt, cries for them in the U.S. '*Quiero irme de aquí porque no puedo ser feliz y no puedo dormir*,' she wrote on the drawing. 'I want to leave from here because I can't be happy and I can't sleep.'"

Now imagine your child drew that. Or another child you care about. We spend so much time and money in our society to protect our children—yet do we fail those who don't look like us, or who weren't lucky enough to be born into as much privilege?

In America, the overarching narrative that we've been taught is that we accept everyone, that we are a melting pot, that this is an equal opportunity land. We've seen that immigration can lead to better jobs, and even job creation for Americans. Yet this is what our current immigration policies look like. We've come a long way from Ellis Island, Angel Island, and that "melting pot" vision of America . . . and many of the changes to that vision of American immigration have happened in the very recent past.

learn ────────────────── 📖

The history of immigration in this country is long and varied—especially depending on what country you came from, what year you came to America, and who was in power when you arrived. We've explored some of this in other chapters (in particular "Gang Violence," Chapter 13, page 131; "Fancy Asians vs. Jungle Asians," Chapter 18, page 179; and "Who Is Latinx Anyway?" Chapter 19, page 191), but let's look briefly at a stretch of time beginning after World War II. With a focus on unification, the U.S. immigration policy was diverse and inclusive of a variety of groups that were newer to the United States. It wasn't perfect, but it was moving in a generally positive direction. In the middle of the civil rights era, President Johnson signed the 1965 Immigration and Naturalization Act into law, which shifted federal immigration legislation away from the 1920s quota system by country of national origin, a system Johnson called "un-American in the highest sense." The Immigration and Naturalization Act set up a system of preferences, which focused on family reunification and allowed naturalized U.S. citizens to sponsor relatives to emigrate to the United States.

Sounds great, right? Families should be together. If someone has been fortunate enough to make their way safely to the United States, they should be able to bring their families along. For some families, that meant they were separated for decades until the family member living in America was able to secure enough funds to bring relatives over. But that was a sacrifice they were willing to make for the American Dream.

In 1980, America's refugee policy changed—for the better— when President Jimmy Carter signed the Refugee Act of 1980, which amended the 1965 Act and raised the limit of refugee visas granted from 17,500 to 50,000 per year, making those numbers exempt from the overall immigration limits; it also established the Office of Refugee Resettlement. Furthermore, and perhaps more importantly, the United States adopted a definition of "refugee" that made it more universal and consistent with the UN Refugee Convention. This change addressed criticism that the United States preferred refugees from some countries (read: Communist) over others.

In 1982, the Immigration Reform and Control Act provided undocumented immigrants who arrived before 1982 the opportunity to apply for permanent resident status before May of 1988. This eventually granted legal status to 3 million people (2.3 of which were Mexican). The Immigration Act of 1990, signed by President

George H. W. Bush, expanded the number of immigration visas allowed as the United States looked for high-skilled workers. In 2001, Congress introduced the DREAM (Development, Relief, and Education for Alien Minors) Act, a policy that would create a path to citizenship for the 2.1 million minors brought illegally to the United States as children; these "DREAMers" had to meet certain conditions, including graduating from a U.S. high school or serving two years in the military. Although the DREAM Act never passed Congress in this form, states passed their own versions to allow for in-state tuition for this group, and in 2012, President Obama announced DACA, a deferred action program that effectively barred DREAMers from deportation. The Obama administration continued to push for large-scale immigration reform, and in 2015, in an attempt to address the global migrant crisis, Secretary of State John Kerry announced that the United States would increase the number of refugees admitted into the country annually from 70,000 to 100,000 by 2017.

MICROAGGRESSION: Assuming a Latinx person is the gardener or house cleaner rather than the homeowner

Immigration appeared to be heading in a specific direction—one which broadly accepted those who needed aid the most, protected those who grew up in this country, and recruited the best and the brightest from all countries. That is, until it wasn't.

Because while these positive steps (as we see them) were happening, let's also remember what was going on. In 2001, we had the 9/11 attacks and experienced significant changes to who we saw as terrorists and threats to our country. In 2010, we had states like Arizona signing their own restrictive immigration laws into effect. And then, in 2017, we had a Trump presidency.

On January 27, 2017, one week after he entered office, President Trump signed an executive order on terrorism prevention that suspended the refugee program for 120 days, banned Syrian refugees indefinitely, and *decreased* the refugee admissions cap to 50,000. It also put the "Muslim Ban" into effect, whereby nationals of Iran, Iraq, Libya, Somalia, Sudan, and Yemen were banned from traveling to the United States for 90 days. In response, a federal judge imposed a nationwide restraining order on the ban—and set off a legal battle. The Supreme Court allowed the third revision of this ban to take effect in June of 2018, ruling that the ban was "within the scope of presidential authority under the Immigration and Nationality Act," and that President Trump's past incendiary statements about Muslims did not undermine the order, which now affected five Muslim-majority countries along with North Korea and Venezuela. Notably, in her dissent, Justice Sonia Sotomayor wrote that "a reasonable observer would conclude that the Proclamation was motivated by anti-Muslim animus." (While this ban was immediately reversed by President Biden upon his taking office, it's important to not forget this part of our recent history.)

April 2018 ended the family unification policies that the United States had worked so hard to legally uphold. Attorney General Jeff Sessions announced a new zero-tolerance policy under which all undocumented immigrants who entered the United States were arrested, and any minors traveling with them were detained separately. This affected several thousand migrant children, many of whom were asylum seekers from Central America, who could be separated from their parents or guardians. Even though President Trump signed an executive order (due to the massive outcry against this policy) ending family separations in June of the same year, the Justice Department maintained that this policy still existed, and reports of mistreatment of migrants in detention centers created new protests and outrage. As of summer 2021, there are still hundreds of children who have not yet been reunited with their families—because the Justice Department effectively can't find the connections between where the kids are and where their parents have been sent. We can't be okay with that.

In 2019, the asylum policy yet again came under attack as the number of Central American migrants attempting to reach the United States appeared to increase. U.S. officials reported close to 600,000 migrants being caught at the southwest border in the first half of 2019, which was roughly twice as many as in 2018. In response, on July 15, 2019, the Trump administration issued a rule that barred migrants "who travel through third countries from seeking asylum in the United States if they have not already sought asylum in the transit country." The effect that this rule has on asylum requests is chilling, and counter to prior policies from the same decade.

Why? Well, remember those makeshift Mexican camps? Now let's say that if you were coming from a Central American country and were passing through Mexico on the way to the United States—you would have to stay in those camps and ask Mexico for asylum before you could even attempt to come to the United States. Because of the high rate of kidnapping, theft, assault, and child abduction attempts in the Remain in Mexico camps, once this was enacted, many asylum seekers chose to go back to the countries that they were trying to flee rather than die in Mexico. And their odds of survival in their home country may be greater than their odds of getting into the United States. Let's say by some miracle they were granted asylum in Mexico. They would then need to file for asylum in the United States. As of September of 2019, there were 47,000 people in the Remain in Mexico program. Less than 10,000 of those had completed their cases—and of those who had completed them, 5,085 cases were denied while 4,471 cases were dismissed without a decision being made—mostly on procedural grounds, according to the newspaper. Only 11 cases, or 0.1 percent of all completed cases, resulted in asylum being granted. ELEVEN CASES. Those odds aren't great. In fact, those odds are terrible and come with high, high risks and inhumane conditions.

Oh, and President Trump attempted to end DACA, but was shut down in 2020 by the Supreme Court as being "arbitrary and capricious" under the Administrative Procedure Act. And just think about this for a second—can you imagine what it would feel like if you were brought here when you were really little, and never knew your "home country," to be suddenly torn from your home in the U.S. and returned to that same "home country" your parents left as adults, with no knowledge or experience of being there? Imagine that happening to your kids.

As we were writing this chapter, yet another immigration issue was up for debate—President Trump's proposed exclusion, without authorization, of undocumented immigrants from the 2020 census numbers that go to the federal count used to award state seats in Congress and the Electoral College. As noted by CBS News, "[t]he U.S. government has always counted most of the country's residents, including noncitizens without legal status, for the purpose of allocating congressional seats. The 14th Amendment requires House seats to be awarded after the government counts 'the whole number of persons in each State.'"

The argument against this Constitutional mandate? That "persons" was not strictly defined in the 14th Amendment—and should exclude immigrants who lack "lawful immigration status." And therein lies the crux and the heart of all four hundred immigration policy and procedural changes, and indeed the recent United States approach to immigration as a whole: immigrants, especially undocumented ones, aren't people.

How troubling is that? Is that consistent with what we may view ourselves to be, with regard to our world status?

act ————————————————————

At this point, you may be feeling like—well, we should be controlling our borders, shouldn't we? When we get too lax, bad things happen. And perhaps that is true—on some levels, and in certain time periods, like active wartime. But categorizing people by race, and barring them from entering our country—that is a real slippery slope. And if we see people as less than people just because they aren't Americans—then we have an even bigger problem that can't be fixed just by writing this book.

But here goes: a few things you can do to better understand where you stand on immigration.

Immigration was on the ballot in 2020, which means that it is an issue currently being discussed in many forums—including in your community. First, find out what the issues are, and where your elected officials stand on them. Is your city a sanctuary city? Are you near a border? Even if your answer to those questions is "No" or "I don't know," immigration still impacts your life, because we're willing to bet that there are many immigrants who are members of your community. (At the very least, you know that neither of us would be here if immigration was restricted or outlawed!)

Second, there are many immigration issues that are soon to be addressed by the Supreme Court—if they weren't already while this book was going to press. We're not saying you need to listen to the legal arguments, but you should be familiar with what those outcomes are. They will affect our immigration policy as a country, how we are seen by the world, and may impact who lives in your community.

Third, there are some great immigration community, policy, and rights groups you can learn from and get involved with as a family. United We Dream is the largest immigrant youth-led nationwide network that is dedicated not only to immigrants' rights but also to stopping unlawful deportation and making sure all voices are heard. RAICES (the Refugee and Immigrant Center for Education and Legal Services) is central in providing free and low-cost legal services to immigrant children, families, and refugees—especially those children who are still separated from their families, and those immigrants and refugees who are being kept at the border, or on the wrong side of the border, due to recent policies. And finally, the Young Center for Immigrant Children's Rights (named after one of their first clients) is the voice for unaccompanied immigrant children, and so desperately needed. Any of these organizations could use your family's support, however you decide to give it.

And fourth, most obviously, if you hear people perpetuating stereotypes of immigrants as anything other than individual case stories, interrupt them and correct them. They are not rapists, thugs, lazy, or illegal. They are human beings who are looking to make a better life for themselves. Give people a chance.

Maybe now, through collective awareness and action, we can truly create the America that we envisioned, that we want to pass on to our kids.

Which Side Will You Stand On?

When we sat down to write this book, it was late 2020, during the darkest weeks when fall hits, the temperature drops, and everything is dying. We were several weeks out from an election that would define this country, and we were months into several pandemics—the obvious one of COVID-19, but the more insidious and longer lasting ones of systemic racism and entrenched hatred as well.

As we wrap up this book, we are now in 2021, several weeks after we witnessed history being made through the swearing in of not only a new president, but of Madam Vice President Kamala Harris, who is not only the first Black and Asian vice president, but also the first female to hold higher office. Through our tears of joy, we saw glimpses of ourselves, our children, and our future in her, and in everything that moment represented.

But as we know—it's not just a moment that defines us. Two weeks prior, we sat in horror as one of the most disgusting displays of White power and White supremacy unfolded before our eyes. We saw insurrectionists storm the Capitol building, hang nooses, wield weapons, and beat people with the American flag while waving the Confederate one. This was not a protest of the kind we saw over the summer, where millions stood up to protect the rights of the underrepresented. This was a violent riot orchestrated by those who sought to *keep* others from the promise of equity, who believed in the lies and conspiracy theories peddled by those who sought to perpetuate the systemic racism and classism and sexism and extreme individualism that America has been founded on. That moment revealed how far we remain from the equity we think we should be closer to by this point. That moment showed us that hatred and fear is still alive and well in 2021, and that we cannot look away. January 6, 2021 showed us what happens if we continue to actively avoid discussing, examining, and reckoning with what it means to be White in America. We have so much work to do.

When you saw both of these moments unfold, maybe you struggled with how to reconcile the two events in your mind. Maybe that's the reason you picked up this book. And now that you've finished this book (or skipped some chapters and ended up here, we see you too!), you may still be asking: Where do we go, when we seem so divided? How can I truly make change?

While we don't have all the answers—nor do we pretend to—we do know this: It is the small things. It's the conversations that start hard and get easier, the interruptions that you don't want to make but are so glad you did, the call that you placed on behalf of the family down the street. It's the lesson you taught your kid and see again when they stand in front of you, proud that they knew what to say and how to stand up for their friend on the playground. These small things are the very things that will make change over time.

This isn't a book to read once. This is a book to read and reference, to keep working through, to open to a specific chapter for a refresher; it's one that you talk about with your kids, friends, and coworkers. This is a book for all of those conversations that we hope you'll have. And if you get stuck, or want more, go download the free PDF workbook we created for you on our website at www.dearwhitewomen.com and use it as a tool to refocus and reengage, because sustaining these conversations *does* take intentional work over time.

As we were reminded several times while writing this book, this isn't just a one and done, or a checklist that we can click through and neatly put to the side while proclaiming we're done. This is about a sustained movement, and all of the diverse voices and styles and brains and bodies that need to be involved. This is about the history that we are living in and creating with every action— or nonaction. And there are only two sides: being anti-racist, or everything else.

Which side will you stand on?

Recommendations

Books

Adult Nonfiction

A Dream Too Big by Caylin Louis Moore

Caste and *The Warmth of Other Suns* by Isabel Wilkerson

Crying in H Mart by Michelle Zauner

Me and White Supremacy by Layla F. Saad

Minor Feelings: An Asian American Reckoning by Cathy Park Hong

Motherhood So White by Nefertiti Austin

My Time Among the Whites by Jennine Capó Crucet

Racism without Racists by Eduardo Bonilla-Silva

Rage Becomes Her by Soraya Chemaly

The Body Is Not an Apology by Sonya Renee Taylor

The Color of Success by Ellen D. Wu

The Good Immigrant edited by Nikesh Shukla and Chimene Suleyman

Thinking Like a Lawyer by Colin Seale

We Should All Be Feminists by Chimamanda Ngozi Adichie

Why Are All the Black Kids Sitting Together in the Cafeteria? (study guide) by Beverly Daniel Tatum

Adult Fiction

Americanah by Chimamanda Ngozi Adichie

An American Marriage by Tayari Jones

Everything I Never Told You by Celeste Ng

Interior Chinatown by Charles Yu

Sabrina & Corina: Stories by Kali Fajardo-Anstine

Such a Fun Age by Kiley Reid

The Vanishing Half by Brit Bennett

The Water Dancer by Ta-Nehisi Coates

Their Eyes Were Watching God by Zora Neale Hurston

There There by Tommy Orange

Children's

All Because You Matter by Tami Charles

Alma and How She Got Her Name by Juana Martinez-Neal

Always Anjali by Sheetal Sheth

Bibbity Bop Barbershop by Natasha Anastasia Tarpley

Black Enough by Ibi Zoboi

black is brown is tan by Arnold Adoff

Don't Ask Me Where I'm From by Jennifer de Leon

I Am Enough by Grace Byers

I Can Make This Promise by Christine Day

Last Stop on Market Street by Matt De La Pena

My Papi Has a Motorcycle by Isabel Quintero

On the Come Up by Angie Thomas

One Crazy Summer (series) by Rita Williams-Garcia

Rosa by Nikki Giovanni

Sing a Song by Kelly Starling Lyons

So Much! by Trish Cooke

The Hate U Give by Angie Thomas

The House on Mango Street by Sandra Cisneros

The Name Jar by Yangsook Choi

The Undefeated by Kwame Alexander

Those Shoes by Maribeth Boelts

Tristan Strong (series) by Kwame Mbalia

When the Beat Was Born by Laban Carrick Hill

Where Are You From? by Yamile Saied Méndez

Your Name Is a Song by Jamilah Thompkins-Bigelow

TV Shows

The Amazing Race

Black-ish

Dear White People

Insecure

Kim's Convenience

Mixed-ish

Never Have I Ever

Nora from Queens

On My Block

Pose

This Is Us

The Upshaws

Vida

When They See Us

Movies

American Skin

Asian Americans

BlackKKlansman

Black Panther

Boyz N the Hood

Crips and Bloods: Made in America

Eyes on the Prize

The Hate U Give

Hidden Figures

I Am Not Your Negro

Just Mercy

MLK/FBI

Selma

She's Gotta Have It (the original and the remake!)

13th

12 Years a Slave

Who Killed Vincent Chin?

Podcasts

The Anti-Racism Daily Podcast

Code Switch

Dear Asian Americans

Dear White Women (of course)

Nice White Parents

The Opt-In

Still Processing

Tamarindo

This Land

Unlocking Us (Dr. Brene Brown's interview with Dr. Ibram X. Kendi)

Vietnamese Boat People

The Woke Desi

You're Wrong About

Sources

Chapter 1

p. 18 Antonio Wint is a Black man: *Voices from Next Door*, Stabio Productions, "Running While Black," video, accessed February 25, 2021, https://www.voicesfromnextdoor.com/videos/running-while-black.

p. 22 we also know that when people are anonymous: Joe Dawson, "Who Is That? The Study of Anonymity and Behavior," *Association for Psychological Science*, March 30, 2018, www.psychologicalscience. org/observer/who-is-that-the-study-of-anonymity-and-behavior.

p. 22 proven to be negative for people's health: Louise C. Hawkley et al., "Loneliness Matters: A Theoretical and Empirical Review of Consequences and Mechanisms," *Annals of Behavioral Medicine* 40, no. 2 (October 2010): 218–227, https://doi.org/10.1007/s12160-010-9210-8.

p. 23 truly does become invisible on a societal level: L. Taylor Phillips et al., "Herd Invisibility: The Psychology of Racial Privilege," *Annals of Behavioral Medicine* 27, no. 3 (2018): 156–162, https://doi.org/10.1177 /0963721417753600.

p. 24 According to a report following the 2010 Census: John R. Logan et al., "The Persistence of Segregation in the Metropolis: New Findings from the 2010 Census," Census brief for Project US2010, March 24, 2011, https://s4.ad.brown.edu/Projects/Diversity/Data/Report /report2.pdf.

p. 24 more than half of American schoolchildren were in racially concentrated districts: Keith Meatto, "Still Separate, Still Unequal: Teaching about School Segregation and Educational Inequality," *New York Times*, May 2, 2019, https://www.nytimes.com/2019/05/02 /learning/lesson-plans/still-separate-still-unequal-teach- ing-about-school-segregation-and-educational-inequality.html.

p. 24 They are less integrated now than in 1970: Rich Benjamin, "Confronting Segregation in the 21st Century," *Forbes*, August 28, 2009, https://www.forbes.com/2009/08/28/integration-segregation -westchester-county-opinions-contributors-rich-benjamin.html?sh =575fef15630b.

p. 24 **A study drawing on contact theory:** James Moody, "Race, School Integration, and Friendship Segregation in America," *American Journal of Sociology* 107, no. 3 (November 2001): 679–716, https://www.journals.uchicago.edu/doi/full/10.1086/338954.

p. 25 **the team at Barna asked 1,000 people:** "U.S. Adults Have Few Friends—and They're Mostly Alike," Barna Access, October 23, 2018, https://www.barna.com/research/friends-loneliness/.

p. 25 **the red shirt/blue shirt experiment:** Dustin Dwyer, "What You Can Learn about Prejudice by Putting Kids in Different Colored Shirts," State of Opportunity, April 3, 2013, https://stateofopportunity.michiganradio.org/post/what-you-can-learn-about-prejudice-putting-kids-different-colored-shirts.

Chapter 2

p. 29 **he watched an animated video on Facebook:** act.tv, Alex Cequea, "Systemic Racism Explained," posted April 26, 2019, https://www.facebook.com/watch/?v=2404667739755980.

p. 31 **In 1619, the privateer White Lion:** History.com editors, "First Enslaved Africans Arrive in Jamestown, Setting the Stage for Slavery in North America," *History*, last updated August 18, 2020, https://www.history.com/this-day-in-history/first-african-slave-ship-arrives-jamestown-colony.

p. 31 **state laws to restrict the former slaves' freedom:** History.com editors, "Black Codes," *History*, last updated January 21, 2021, https://www.history.com/topics/black-history/black-codes.

p. 32 **Then, in 1934, the Federal Housing Administration:** "1934: Federal Housing Administration Created," The Fair Housing Center of Greater Boston, accessed February 25, 2021, https://www.bostonfairhousing.org/timeline/1934-FHA.html.

p. 33 **Despite *Shelley v. Kraemer,* a 1948 case:** Shelley v. Kraemer, 334 U.S. 1, 68 S. (Ct. 836 1948), https://www.lexisnexis.com/community/casebrief/p/casebrief-shelley-v-kraemer.

p. 33 **A study by the National Community Reinvestment Coalition:** Bruce Mitchell et al., "HOLC 'Redlining' Maps: The Persistent Structure of Segregation and Economic Inequality," National Community Reinvestment Coalition, March 20, 2018, https://ncrc.org/holc/.

Chapter 3

p. 39 **according to the Universal Declaration:** Universal Declaration of Human Rights, United Nations, accessed February 28, 2021, https://www.un.org/en/universal-declaration-human-rights/index.html.

p. 42 Ronald Inglehart and Pippa Norris have studied: Ronald F. Ingle-hart, "Giving Up on God: The Global Decline of Religion," *Foreign Affairs*, September/October 2020, https://www.foreignaffairs.com /articles/world/2020-08-11/religion-giving-god.

p. 42 for which we have data: *The World Values Survey* database, https://www.foreignaffairs.com/articles/world/2020-08-11/reli-gion-giving-god?utm_medium=email_notifications&utm_source=reg _confirmation&utm_campaign=reg_guestpass

p. 42 Since the 1990s, the Republican Party has sought: Ronald F. Inglehart, "Why Is Religion Suddenly Declining?" *Oxford University Press's Academic Insights for the Thinking World*, December 7, 2020, https://blog.oup.com/2020/12/why-is-religion-suddenly-declining/.

p. 44 many studies show that being open to listening to other people: Francesca Gino, "Disagreement Doesn't Have to be Divisive," *Harvard Business Review*, November 16, 2020, https://hbr.org/2020/11 /disagreement-doesnt-have-to-be-divisive.

p. 44 one of the studies mentioned above: Gino, "Disagreement."

p. 45 Research from the Brookings Institution states: Thomas Caroth-ers et al., "Democracies Divided: The Global Challenge of Political Polarization," *Brookings*, https://www.brookings.edu/wp-content /uploads/2019/04/democracies-divided_introduction-1.pdf

p. 45 Over the past four decades, the chilly chasm of negative senti-ment: May Wong, "When It Comes to Polarization across the Globe, America Leads the Way," *Palo Alto Online*, January 20, 2020, https:// www.paloaltoonline.com/news/2020/01/20/study-when-it-comes -to-polarization-across-the-globe-american-leads-the-way.

p. 45 political talk in the workplace: "1 in 4 Employees Negatively Affected by Political Talk at Work This Election Season," American Psychological Association, September 14, 2016, https://www.apa.org /news/press/releases/2016/09/employees-political-talk.

Chapter 4

p. 50 An article from Learning for Justice: Zaretta Hammond, "Is Implicit Bias Racist?" *Learning for Justice*, June 1, 2015, https:// www.learningforjustice.org/magazine/is-implicit-bias-racist.

p. 50 amid the total universe of all the people we know: Emily Badger, "Scientists May Have Decoded Your Social Circle," *Bloomberg CityLab*, January 7, 2014, https://www.bloomberg.com/news/articles/2014 -01-07/scientists-may-have-decoded-your-social-circle.

p. 50 For Americans, that core has, on average, 3.4 people: Daniel Cox et al., "Race, Religion, and Political Affiliation of Americans' Core